SMART WOMEN LIVE RICHLY

SMART WOMEN LIVE RICHLY

HELENE LERNER

LIBRARY TALES PUBLISHING

Library Tales Publishing
www.LibraryTalesPublishing.com
www.Facebook.com/LibraryTalesPublishing

For general information on our other products and services, please contact our Customer Care Department at 1-800-754-5016, or fax 917-463-0892. For technical support, please visit www.LibraryTalesPublishing.com

Library Tales Publishing also publishes its books in a variety of electronic formats. Every content that appears in print is available in electronic books.

9 7 9 8 8 9 4 4 1 0 4 2 5

Printed in the United States of America

Get Ready to Embark on an Amazing Journey...

You are about to travel to places your heart has long desired. You have developed talents and gifts that are uniquely yours, supporting you in *Living Richly*. Now is the moment to use them fully and receive opportunities beyond your wildest dreams.

PUBLISHER'S NOTE

*M*any of the stories shared in this book are not direct accounts of specific individuals. Instead, they represent a thoughtfully crafted blend of experiences from the author's extensive work with colleagues, clients, friends, and acquaintances. These narratives are composites designed to reflect common themes, struggles, and break-throughs encountered by many people on their journey toward personal growth and transformation.

While the details of each story may have been adapted for clarity and impact, the underlying lessons, emotions, and challenges are rooted in real-life experiences. They are powerful examples of how individuals can overcome obstacles, shift their mindsets, and create meaningful, lasting change. The goal of these stories is not to recount exact events but to inspire, guide, and offer relatable insights that can help readers unlock their potential for abundance and personal fulfillment.

PREFACE

UNLOCKING YOUR ABUNDANT LIFE

*L*et me ask you something: Are you ready to transform your life by changing what you *have* and redefining what you *value*? What I'm about to share with you isn't surface-level advice or quick-fix solutions; it's the foundation for a more prosperous, fuller, and more abundant life. This is your invitation to step into a new way of living that aligns your deepest desires with your daily reality.

This book will reveal principles that may feel familiar but haven't yet become part of your way of being. Why? Because the truth isn't always easy. But here's the good news: Everything changes once you start living with intention and focus, following the leanings of your heart. I've helped thousands of people break free from limiting beliefs, and now it's your turn. You're here because you're ready. You're ready to reclaim the abundance that's been waiting for you all along.

I know this journey firsthand. Several years ago, I hit my breaking point. I looked successful on the outside but felt empty on the inside. My career was impactful, but I focused too much on external achievements. When I didn't reach those benchmarks, I blamed myself, my circumstances, anything but the real issue.

Here is the truth I discovered: Financial success, while important, is only one piece of the puzzle. Wealth is hollow without inner peace, joy, and purpose. This isn't a book about *making money*—it's a guide to cultivating a *Prosperity Mindset*. When you do that, everything flows: peace, joy, abundance—and, yes, financial growth, too.

It starts with gratitude, self-compassion, and living fully in the present moment. It is about building relationships with love and authenticity while tapping into a higher power—whatever that means to you. Some of the richest moments of my life have had nothing to do with money. Like laughing with my great-nephew Rowan (a toddler now) or hearing my team say they trust me because they know I care; those treasures make life genuinely abundant.

But let's be honest, most of us miss these riches. We're so wrapped up in our Mad Mind-Chatter, the constant stream of thoughts telling us we're not enough, don't have enough, that we can't stop to see the blessings right in front of us. So, how do you make the shift? Winning the lottery won't do it. Neither will getting that big promotion or inheriting a mansion. Those things are nice, but they don't create happiness. Genuine abundance comes from appreciating and nurturing what you already have and value most.

In this book, you'll find practices, exercises, and questions designed to silence that inner noise and clarify what *Living Richly* means for you. Together, we'll create a roadmap for living your richest life. You'll learn to trust your heart as the compass it was meant to be.

And here's what's waiting for you on the other side:

- Laughter, joy, and fun as you go about your day.
- Deeper, more meaningful relationships.
- A profound connection to your higher power.
- A sense of peace and security that no external circumstance can shake.
- A wellspring of compassion for yourself and others.

Claim your birthright to love and be loved, to share your unique talents, and to feel secure, healthy, and connected. You deserve a life that truly lights you up. The real question is—are you ready to say yes? If you are, let's begin.

The First Key is about *letting go*. You're going to release the beliefs and behaviors that no longer serve you, clearing the way for new possibilities. But first, it's time to take the *Living Richly Quiz* and get honest about what's holding you back. You have already taken the first courageous step by picking up this book and choosing to explore what it means to live richly. That takes guts. Facing the truth about ourselves is never easy, and it's far simpler to point fingers at people or circumstances when life doesn't go our way. I know because I've been there. But blaming gets you nowhere. Transformation begins when we turn inward and take responsibility for how we show up in our own lives.

So, let's clarify what *Living Richly* means to you. What are your true feelings about wealth, abundance, and fulfillment? I invite you to dig deep and answer honestly, because that is where the shift begins.

LIVING RICHLY QUIZ

1. What does *"Living Richly"* mean to you?

  a. It means living fully and experiencing the best in life.
  b. It is tied to how much money I have.
  c. It is connected to money and more.

2. Do you believe that *Living Richly* is primarily dependent on money?

  a. No.
  b. Yes.
  c. Maybe.

3. How does letting people know the "real you" enter into living a prosperous lifestyle?

    a. When I am myself, my life feels expansive.
    b. It doesn't enter into it because it's all about having money.
    c. I struggle with letting people know me.

4. What brings you the greatest joy?

    a. Being with people I love.
    b. Money.
    c. A combination of things.

5. What creates a poverty mentality?

    a. Not appreciating all I have.
    b. Not having enough money.
    c. I'm not sure—I feel poorer than I would like.

6. What do you think impresses people?

    a. How kind you are.
    b. Definitely money and material things.
    c. A combination of both.

7. What makes people joyful?

    a. Being able to enjoy the little things in life.
    b. Having wealth.
    c. A combination of both.

8. If money was not an issue, what would your life be like?

    a. A little easier than it is now, but I am grateful for all I have.
    b. Everything would be wonderful.
    c. A little better than it is now, but I'm not sure how much.

Take a moment to add up the number of **A**, **B**, and **C** responses. Which letter came up most often for you?

- If your answers were mostly **A's**, you likely already feel prosperous and recognize that true wealth comes from within.
- If you had mostly **B's**, you might put too much emphasis on money as the solution to all your challenges.
- And if you landed on mostly **C's**, you may feel conflicted about wealth and unsure how intangible elements like joy, love, and gratitude fit into your definition of abundance.

Now that you've taken the quiz, pause and reflect. Did anything new come to light? Maybe you noticed some thought patterns or habits that aren't serving you. Awareness is always the first step to change. When you see what's holding you back, you can break free from the beliefs and behaviors that keep you stuck.

The chapters ahead are packed with tools and stories to help you uncover what might be blocking your path to abundance. You'll find journal prompts to help you dig deeper, practical exercises to shift your mindset, and inspiring examples of people who have made these changes themselves. Together, we'll work to silence that constant mental chatter—the "Mad Mind-Talk" that keeps you trapped—and replace it with clarity and purpose.

Let me leave you with this: You have the power to create the life you desire. That power is already within you, waiting to be unleashed. The first step is to let go of a scarcity mindset and embrace the possibilities ahead.

FOR YOUR JOURNAL

1. What did you discover about yourself after taking the quiz? What harmful habit are you ready to let go of?

2. What is lacking in your life right now that you would like to manifest? Be specific.

CONTENTS

THE FIRST KEY

GIVING UP

When we let go of people, places, and things that no longer serve us,
we open ourselves up to immense joy and abundance.

CHAPTER 1

LETTING GO OF A POVERTY MINDSET

When we release destructive habits, we create space for abundance to flow into our lives.

*L*et me ask you something: If you don't know the terrain, why would you trust the "yellow-brick road" to lead you to Oz? The same applies to your mindset. If you've been following the wrong path—believing in lack, fear, or limitation—it's no wonder you haven't reached the abundant life you desire. But here's the good news: Today, you're stepping off that misguided path and onto a new one.

You've already taken the first step by engaging in this process. That takes courage. It's not easy to face the qualities we don't like about ourselves. Most people avoid this kind of introspection because it's uncomfortable. But facing discomfort is a sign of strength. By flexing your inner muscles, you're already on your way to transformation. And yes, like any exercise routine, there might be some initial pain. That's okay; it's proof you're growing and stepping out of your comfort zone.

Change begins by simply showing up and taking responsibility for your mindset. Now, let's go a step further.

Take a moment to reflect:

- Do you feel like you have enough material wealth and possessions to live well?
- Do you wake up most days excited about the twenty-four hours ahead?
- Are you genuinely enjoying your life and appreciating what you already have?

If you answered "no" to any of these questions, you're likely experiencing a sense of deprivation. You might find yourself longing for something external to fill an internal void. This feeling of lack isn't just yours. For many, it's a legacy passed down from one generation to the next. Think about your family's history with money and abundance. Chances are, if you're carrying a poverty mentality, your relatives struggle with the same.

Here's the price you pay for this mindset: dissatisfaction, a lackluster life, and constant longing. The good news? You don't have to stay stuck. There's a way out, a road less traveled—from poverty to prosperity.

SHIFTING FROM POVERTY TO PROSPERITY: A ROAD LESS TRAVELED

This shift is possible. It starts with awareness and a willingness to do the work. And yes, a little help from your higher power doesn't hurt. What does it take to make this shift? Reframing, or transforming negative thoughts into positive ones.

Now, you might be thinking, "Easier said than done." And you're right. But let me break it down. The first step is understanding why we cling to negativity. It's familiar, isn't it? Obsessing over fears or limitations gives us a false sense of control. At least we know what to expect when we let anxiety and doubt run the show. But here's the problem: This cycle keeps you stuck.

To create an abundant life, you must shift from *negative mind talk* —what I call Mad Mind-Chatter—to *positive heart talk.* *

Think of it this way: your body has two major control centers—the critical mind and the heart. The mind can create chaos, but the heart grounds you in truth. When you let your heart lead, you tap into your inner wisdom.

Yes, this shift feels risky. Growth is an uncomfortable but necessary component of change. I encourage you to adopt this mantra:

Get comfortable with the uncomfortable.

For me, connecting to something greater than my ego—what I call the critical mind—makes this process easier. Call it God, the Universe, a Benevolent Force, or simply the highest part of me—this higher power resides in your heart and is always available to guide you.

A PERSONAL EXAMPLE

Let me share a story from my early career. One of my first jobs was in sales, and I'll be honest, I hated it. I had this image of salespeople as sleazy manipulators—people smoking cigars around a poker table, scheming how to get customers to buy things they didn't need. With that mindset, guess what happened? I wasn't making any sales.

Then, a friend handed me a book that changed my perspective: *The Greatest Salesman in the World* by Og Mandino. That book reframed every-thing for me. I stopped seeing salespeople as manipulators and started seeing them as being of service to others. Suddenly, I realized I could make an impact by helping people find solutions they truly needed.

That simple mindset shift—from "salespeople manipulate customers" to "salespeople serve customers"—transformed my performance. Within months, I became the top performer in my department, breaking records that had stood for years.

---

* Helene Lerner, *The Confidence Myth: Why Women Undervalue Their Skills and How to Get Over It* (California: Berrett-Koehler, 2015), 11.

The lesson? Changing your mindset changes your results. It's not magic; it's a choice.

WHAT NEGATIVE MIND-CLUTTER ARE YOU BELIEVING IN?

When we hear the word "clutter," we often think of a physical mess—piles of papers, overflowing closets, or that drawer we avoid opening. But clutter isn't limited to something physical. Our minds can be just as packed with junk—negative thoughts, limiting beliefs, and toxic narratives. And just like cleaning your home, decluttering your mind creates space for growth, clarity, and new opportunities.

Today, you're starting the process of clearing that mental clutter. This isn't just an exercise—it's a step toward living with intention and freedom. Begin by taking the *Mind Clutter Inventory* below. Share some of your insights with a trusted friend.

MIND CLUTTER INVENTORY

1. Are you generally unforgiving toward people who disappoint you in your personal life or at work?
2. Do you feel victimized, overlooked, or unfairly treated by supervisors or colleagues?
3. Do you often rehash petty grievances, keeping them alive in your mind?
4. Do you catch yourself telling subtle lies but continuing anyway?
5. Do you feel superior or inferior to others, struggling to see yourself as an equal?
6. Do you compare yourself to others and, in doing so, discount your accomplishments?

As you reflect on these questions, you might recognize patterns that have been limiting you in ways you weren't even aware of. Don't judge yourself for these realizations; awareness is the first step to change. The goal is to let go of these beliefs and behaviors so you can lead a richer, more fulfilling life.

ATTITUDES THAT HOLD YOU BACK—AND HOW TO OVERCOME THEM

Let's examine the most common attitudes that clutter our minds and discuss what you can do to clear them.

1. Blame and Lack of Forgiveness

- **How it holds you back:** Blaming others and holding grudges keep you stuck in the past, tethered to negativity. It drains your energy and leaves no room for growth.
- **Overcoming strategy:** Take a moment to understand what motivates the people you have a problem with. Practicing forgiveness doesn't excuse their behavior; it frees you from the burden of resentment.

2. Feeling Like a Victim

- **How it holds you back:** Believing you're a victim strips you of your power. It's like handing over the keys to your life and letting someone else drive.
- **Overcoming strategy:** Take responsibility for your role in the situation. This doesn't mean blaming yourself; it means owning your choices and learning from them.

3. Holding on to Petty Grievances

- **How it holds you back:** Rehashing small slights keeps you focused on what's wrong instead of what's possible. It's a mental treadmill—you're running but going nowhere.
- **Overcoming strategy:** Channel that energy into something productive. Focus on the task at hand and the goals you want to achieve.

4. Telling Subtle Lies

- **How it holds you back:** Dishonesty, even in small doses, creates a divide between you and your authentic self. It erodes trust—both with others and yourself.
- **Overcoming strategy:** Start becoming aware of when you're being dishonest, no matter how small the lie. Pause and consciously shift toward the truth.

5. Believing Money Will Buy Happiness

- **How it holds you back:** Money is a tool, not a source of fulfillment. Believing it's the answer to your problems leads to a never-ending chase for "enough."
- **Overcoming strategy:** Recognize that money is only part of the equation. Take risks in other areas of your life, such as relationships, personal growth, and creative endeavors.

LET IT GO

Clearing the Mad Mind-Chatter isn't about perfection. It's about progress. Each time you recognize and release a limiting thought, you make space for something new—peace, clarity, and opportunities. Letting go of mental clutter leaves you open and ready to embrace the abundance that's already waiting for you.

Repeat this mantra as often as you need:

Let it go. Let it all go.

REAL-LIFE TRANSFORMATIONS: LETTING GO OF THE LIES

Delores is a perfect example of how letting go of mental clutter and shifting your mindset can transform your life. A dedicated yoga instructor with a packed client list, Delores appeared to be thriving professionally. But beneath the surface, she wasn't happy. Her life revolved around work, paying bills, and meeting responsibilities. She avoided taking chances, whether in dating, traveling, or even letting loose for a night of fun.

Her turning point? A big birthday was on the horizon, and her adult son once again asked her to celebrate at a fun local hotspot, a request she'd declined for years. This time, she said *yes*.

When I spoke to her afterward, she was glowing. She shared how she'd eaten ribs for the first time (yes, ribs!) and danced until one in the morning. That night wasn't just a celebration—it was a declaration. Delores vowed to fully embrace life, starting with her long-neglected passion for traveling.

When I asked her what had shifted, she said, "Making money was my life, but I realized I'd been putting off the things that truly mattered to me. I wasn't taking any chances. Another instructor, close to my age, recently passed away, prompting me to reflect on my priorities."

Delores had spent years believing her Mad Mind-Chatter: *"Making lots of money will give me a good life."* But her subtle shift was this: *"Making money is important, but a good life is about more than that."*

What's remarkable is that Delores didn't need millions to start *Living Richly*. She simply needed the willingness to say *yes* to joy.

WHEN MIND CLUTTER STRIKES MOST

For many of us, the voice of Mad Mind-Chatter gets loudest when there's no urgency—when life feels like it's on autopilot. We're too busy dealing with immediate challenges during a crisis to obsess over negative thoughts. But when things are calm, that inner voice starts spinning its web: reasons we can't act, excuses for why we won't succeed, or fears that hold us back.

Take Sally's story, for instance.

Sally had been an executive assistant to the vice president of marketing for two years. She aspired to become a marketing associate and even took courses at a local college to improve her skills. But nothing was changing. She felt stuck, bored, and uninspired at work.

Her problem wasn't a lack of opportunity; it was fear. Deep down, Sally was afraid that if she took a chance, she wouldn't succeed. Instead of facing that fear, she stayed safe, telling herself little lies: *"It's not the right time,"* or *"It's not going to happen anyway."*

One night, Sally went to dinner with her good friend Kelly, who reminded her of a time when she was braver. Kelly brought up the months Sally first moved to the city—no job, apartment, or safety net. Sally had slept on Kelly's couch but never gave up. Within two months, she had a job and her own place to live.

That conversation was the spark Sally needed. She realized she had let her Mad Mind-Chatter convince her she couldn't move forward. But remembering her past success reignited her confidence. With Kelly's encouragement, Sally flipped the script. Instead of thinking, *"If I try, I'll fail,"* she started telling herself, *"I've grown, I've gained new skills, and I'm ready for the next step."*

Sally began networking outside of her company, seeking new opportunities which led to her landing an exciting promotion.

WHAT'S HOLDING YOU BACK?

Both Delores and Sally had one thing in common: their limiting beliefs were based on fear, and that fear kept them from stepping into their fullest potential. But when they decided to challenge those beliefs, their lives changed.

This isn't about making a massive leap overnight. It's about recognizing the stories you've been telling yourself, the ones that hold you back—and taking one small, courageous step toward change, and then another, and another.

Living Richly Practice
It Can Work Out in the End

Life is full of moments that challenge us to step out of our comfort zones, confront our fears, and embrace new opportunities. It's not easy—there are years of habits, doubts, and beliefs to contend with—but it's always worth it.

Take a moment to reflect. When was the last time you believed you wouldn't get what you wanted, but it worked out in the end? Why do you think it worked out? Did you reach out for help? If so, who supported you? And most importantly, how did you grow from that experience?

SHIFTING THE LENS OF REGRET

As you start to shift your thinking, remorse might creep in. You may find yourself asking, *"Why didn't I do this sooner? I've wasted so much time."* Our *Smart Women Live Richly* survey showed how easy it is to get caught up in staring back at the past. When asked about situations where fear kept them from taking action, over 40% of respondents said they spent time regretting that.

But here's the thing: Regret, when handled with care, can be a powerful motivator. It shows us what we don't want to repeat and spurs us to make better choices moving forward.

It's best to glance back, not stare. Shame doesn't help. Use the past as a guidepost, not a jail cell. Think of regret as a marker for growth, not as something that defines you.

For instance, Sally, who struggled with leaving a stagnant job, could have easily dwelled on how long she stayed in a position she'd outgrown. Instead, she asked herself a better question: *"What fear was holding me back?"* By naming it—fear of starting over and not fitting into a new company—she could move on. She shifted her thinking from *"It's too late to leave"* to *"I've gained so much here, but it's time to move on. Yes, there's a learning curve in a new job, but I can handle it."*

This mindset shift is the foundation of *Living Richly*. The more you practice it, the easier it becomes to silence that Mad Mind-Chatter and embrace the possibilities ahead.

THE LESSONS IN TIMING

Sometimes, even when we're ready, the change we want doesn't happen right away. Sound familiar? Maybe you've worked hard, made progress, and still find yourself waiting for results. Frustrating, isn't it? I've been there.

When I lost most of my weight in my late 20s, I hit a plateau with the last ten pounds. I was impatient, frustrated, and ready to give up. But looking back, I realized there was a reason for the delay. Those months weren't wasted; they were teaching me something more profound. I learned to set boundaries, to say "no" to things that didn't serve me, and to become comfortable with a new, more attractive version of myself.

It's the same with Cindy's story. A talented fashion designer, Cindy loved her work but couldn't refuse others' demands. Overwhelmed and exhausted, her dream of traveling seemed out of reach. It wasn't until a colleague challenged her to look at why she felt *obligated* to help everyone else that Cindy made a shift. She began saying "no" to requests that drained her energy and finally carved out time for herself.

Cindy's transformation didn't happen overnight. It took persistence, discomfort, and patience. But when she finally did step into her power, she found the space to travel and live the adventurous life she'd been dreaming of.

THE POWER OF DIVINE TIMING

There's a concept that has guided me time and time again: *divine timing.* It's the understanding that things unfold not on our schedule but when the timing is right. One of my mentors, a high-level corporate executive, taught me this lesson. She was ready to roll out a transformative program for her employees, but instead of rushing it, she took six months to prepare her leadership team. The result? A successful launch.

Delays often have a purpose. They allow us to grow, to prepare, and to become ready for the opportunities ahead. When we shift our perspective to see delay as preparation for something better, we create space for trust and abundance.

Living Richly Practice
Shift Your Perspective

Take a moment to reflect on your own life. Think back to a time when you wanted to move forward but had to wait. What was the situation? Who was involved? How did the waiting period prepare you for what was to come?

Write down your insights and share them with someone you trust. Often, the lessons we learn in waiting are just as valuable as the outcome itself.

TAKE THE 'YES' CHALLENGE

This week, say *yes* to something new. If an opportunity arises in your personal life, embrace it. At work, if you have a creative idea, act on it. Take one step, and then another. The momentum you build by saying *yes* will open doors you didn't even know were there.

It's never too late to create the life you want. The first step is letting go of the habits and beliefs that are holding you back, such as a poverty mentality. In the next chapter, we'll explore strategies for shedding false personas that might be blocking your abundance.

CHAPTER TAKEAWAYS

- It's almost impossible to live richly when you're stuck in dissatisfaction.
- To create an abundant life, shift from negative *Mad Mind-Chatter* to positive *heart talk.*
- Mind clutter is loudest when life is quiet. Crisis often forces us into the present moment.
- Regret can be a motivator, but don't dwell on it—use it as a guidepost for better decisions.
- Change takes time, and that's okay. Delays often prepare us for what's to come.

NUGGET FROM THE HEART

When you move through your fears and say *yes* to the opportunities before you, life opens up beyond your wildest dreams.

FOR YOUR JOURNAL

1. Are you as patient as you'd like to be, or do you demand things happen on your timeline? If the latter, what are you afraid of?
2. Do you believe in *divine timing*? If so, what does that mean to you? Can you think of a time in your life when it happened?

CHAPTER 2

LETTING GO OF THE FALSE YOU

Courage allows the real you to step forward and stand in your truth, whether or not people approve.

Too often, we bend ourselves out of shape trying to meet others' expectations. We put on masks, play roles, and pretend to be someone we're not just to gain approval. But here's the truth: it's exhausting being an imposter. It's like carrying a heavy burden, constantly looking over your shoulder, wondering when someone will discover the "real" you.

This tendency to be inauthentic often starts early in life. I remember being called "Happy Helenie" as a little girl. My unspoken job was to make people feel good. And so, I pretended to be happy, even when I wasn't. I learned to read minds, to anticipate what others wanted, and act accordingly. By the time I was a teenager, I had perfected the art of playing it cool, trying to come across as sophisticated and worldly. But my so-called friends weren't buying it.

By my twenties, the charade was unraveling. I was deeply unhappy, and nothing seemed to work. I reached such a low point that I nearly ended my life. Eventually, as an obese adult, I found support to lose weight. But keeping it off required far more than diet and exercise—it required authenticity.

To maintain my progress, I had to confront the real me. I had to understand and be honest about my feelings, ask for what I needed, and learn to say *no* when necessary. I had to stop people-pleasing in search of friendship or approval. It was terrifying and messy—full of trial and error—but it was also freeing. I stepped out of my comfort zone, and over time, I learned this simple but profound truth: I can't please everyone, and trying to do so is a waste of energy.

To be authentic, you must know what you think, feel what you feel, and act accordingly. It's not about perfection; it's about alignment.

Your story might not be as extreme as mine, but if you find yourself distorting the truth or compromising your values to gain approval, some adjustments are in order. The first step is awareness. Take the following quiz to see how much others' opinions influence your actions.

QUIZ: ARE YOU A PEOPLE-PLEASER?

1. When I am ready to do something out of the ordinary, I...

    a. Do it!
    b. See what others think about it first.
    c. Don't do anything because I'm not sure if it's the right decision.

2. A friend calls and tells you that your decision to move across the country is a mistake. You...

    a. Say, "It's the right move for me—I've thought about it a lot."
    b. Get defensive and respond, *"You're probably right."*
    c. Torment yourself because you are unsure if you're making the right decision.

3. Your boss suggests you're not ready for a promotion. You...

a. Try to convince him you are (to no avail), so you set up an interview for a position at another company because you believe you're already.
b. Agree and pull back.
c. Feel stuck and conflicted.

4. Your mother-in-law is fussy (nothing is ever good enough for her), and she's coming over for dinner. You...

a. Cook a delicious meal and look forward to serving it, regardless of her reaction.
b. Feel angry and defensive, assuming she'll criticize at least one dish.
c. Regret going to the trouble, thinking, *"It's just not worth the aggravation."*

How Did You Do?

Total up your A, B, and C answers.

- If you answered mostly **A's**, you're likely confident in your decisions and not overly influenced by what others say.
- If you answered mostly **B's**, you're probably swayed by others' opinions and may struggle to stand your ground.
- If you answered mostly **C's**, you likely feel conflicted and uncertain about balancing your desires with others' expectations.

Take a moment to reflect: Did you learn anything new about yourself?

WHEN WE CROSS THE LINE

We've all had moments when insecurity gets the best of us. Times when we subvert our authentic selves to impress others or avoid conflict. Do any of these examples resonate with you?

- You say *yes* to something you don't want to do, fearing you'll disappoint someone if you decline.
- You act agreeable in a meeting, even when you have a differing opinion, to avoid making waves.
- You buy an expensive gift for someone, not because it's what you want to give but because you're worried they'll judge a more honest choice.

These behaviors don't just drain your energy; they erode your self-worth. Over time, they teach you that who you are isn't enough. But here's the good news: You can break the cycle.

SHIFT YOUR MINDSET WHEN INSECURITY TAKES OVER

We've all had moments when we don't act true to form, but we can shift our mindset and reframe our thoughts.

Consider these scenarios:

Scenario One:

You walk into a room full of strangers and immediately scan for reactions. You catch yourself thinking, *"Are they noticing me? Do I look attractive?"* If heads turn, you feel validated, even confident. But if no one looks, your mood plummets, and self-doubt creeps in.

Reframe:

Pause for a moment and ask yourself, *"Why does it matter what they think? How do I feel about myself right now?"* Your sense of worth shouldn't hinge on the reactions of people you don't even know. Instead, focus on confidently walking into that room, knowing you belong there regardless of external validation.

Scenario Two:

You're out to lunch with a good friend, and she's brought along someone new—a colleague. As they exchange side comments and laugh, you feel left out. Your mind spirals: *"Does she care more about her than me? Am I not interesting enough?"*

Reframe:

Shift the focus inward and ask yourself, *"Do I enjoy this new person's company? Am I curious about who she is?"* Instead of assuming exclusion, lean into the moment. Engage, ask questions, and decide if this is someone you'd want to know better. Remember, feeling left out is often a story we tell ourselves, not the reality.

Scenario Three:

A new colleague joins your team. During the weekly meeting, you notice that his presentation skills are strong. You start to compare yourself to him and feel like you are falling short. Your mind fixates on it, so much that you don't hear a critical comment your boss makes.

Reframe:

Flip the narrative. Consider that the new hire is probably just as concerned about making a good impression. Instead of focusing on comparisons, tap into your strengths. *"How can I support him? How can I show up as a leader?"* You'll be building a better working relationship and earning respect if you do.

WHEN EGO RUNS THE SHOW

In each scenario, the common thread is an overfocus on others' opinions. This unhealthy, ego-driven mindset pulls us away from joy, connection, and authenticity—leaving no room for us to simply be ourselves.

But these aren't the only ways insecurity shows up. Think about the times you've said "yes" when you really wanted to say "no." Maybe you agreed to a favor you didn't have time for, fearing you'd disappoint someone. Or you went along with a decision you didn't believe in just to avoid conflict. Each time we prioritize others' opinions over our own truth, we undermine our authenticity.

Learning to say "no" with conviction is one of the most empowering steps you can take toward living a more authentic life.

Living Richly Practice
Saying "No" and Meaning It

1. **Pause and Reflect:** When faced with a request, pause before responding. Ask yourself, *"Is this something I really want to do? Do I have the capacity for this?"* The answer is "no".

2. **Acknowledge Your Feelings:** If saying *"no"* makes you uncomfortable, recognize it without judgment. It's okay to feel uneasy; it means you're stepping into new territory.

3. **Respond with Kindness:** You don't need to overexplain or justify your decision. A simple, *"I'm sorry, I can't commit to that right now,"* is enough.

4. **Stand Firm:** Remember, you're not responsible for managing others' reactions to your boundaries. Saying *"no"* is about honoring your time, energy, and priorities.

LIVING FROM YOUR STRENGTHS

When we stop seeking validation from others and begin to trust ourselves, we open the door to greater confidence and more profound joy. It's not about being perfect or never feeling unsure; it's about catching yourself in those moments and choosing a new path.

The next time you feel yourself slipping into self-doubt or people-pleasing, take a breath. Reframe the situation. Ask yourself: *"Am I acting from my strength or my insecurities?"* The more you practice this shift, the more natural it becomes to show up as the real you.

Living Richly Practice
Saying "No" with an Alternative

Boundaries are the foundation of authentic relationships. Learn to say *"yes"* when you mean it and *"no"* when you need to protect your energy because there is too much on your plate.

Saying *"no"* doesn't mean shutting people out or abandoning compassion. When you can't accommodate someone's request, try offering an alternative. For instance, if a friend asks for your help and your schedule is packed, tell them that while you can't commit, someone else might be a better fit. You could say, *"I can't take this on right now, but you might want to ask [Name]. They'd be great for this."* This approach respects your limits while still being helpful.

The ability to set boundaries extends beyond simply saying *"no."* It also requires identifying habits that undermine your ability to live authentically. Let's explore some of these patterns, along with real-life examples of how they can manifest.

WHEN YOU NEED TO BE RIGHT

The need to be right is a trap that changes how we interact with others. It can turn meaningful conversations into battles where the only goal is to win. In the process, we lose empathy, damage relationships, and miss opportunities for connection.

Carli's story illustrates this perfectly. She was known for her sharp wit and unwavering stance in arguments. One time, she purchased tickets for a rock concert, covering the cost for her friends upfront. While it was agreed that everyone would pay her back at the event, one friend—tight on cash —asked to pay her at the end of the month. Instead of showing understanding, Carli lashed out, embarrassing the friend in front of the group.

Carli's need to prove a point outweighed her compassion. Although she didn't need the money immediately, her reaction created unnecessary tension and hurt feelings. It wasn't about the money but about needing to feel in control and validated.

The next time you encounter a similar situation, pause and ask yourself if being right is worth the cost of the relationship. Often, graciousness occurs when we let the argument go and choose understanding over victory.

WHEN YOU NEED TO DO IT ALL YOURSELF

Taking on too much without asking for help can lead to burnout, resentment, and strained relationships. Often, we fall into this trap because we feel it's our duty or fear that others won't step up if we don't. The result? We become martyrs, silently resentful while pretending to handle everything without too much stress.

Marie, a grandmother, loved spending time with her twin grandchildren. Every weekday, she picked them up from school, gave them snacks, and waited until her daughter Bev returned from work. While she adored the twins, Bev's increasingly late arrivals pushed Marie beyond her limits. Instead of addressing the issue directly, Marie expressed her frustration through sarcasm. Her tone created an uncomfortable atmosphere for the children, and the tension between her and Bev finally erupted in an argument.

In the heat of the moment, Bev said she'd hire a full-time babysitter, which wasn't what Marie wanted at all. Realizing she hadn't been honest about her needs, Marie apologized and said, *"I love spending time with the twins, but five hours a day is too much for me. I can manage a few more late nights, but if it continues, we'll need to find extra help alongside what I can do."* This honest conversation allowed them to find a solution that worked for both.

Marie's story is a reminder that asking for help doesn't mean failure. It means valuing your time and energy enough to protect them. When we communicate our limits honestly, we strengthen our relationships rather than weaken them.

WHEN YOU NEED TO BE IN CONTROL

The need to control situations—or people—often stems from insecurity. We think that by managing everything, we'll feel more secure. But the truth is, control is an illusion. No matter how hard we try, we can't dictate others' actions or outcomes. The only thing we can control is ourselves.

Ruth learned this the hard way. Her husband's excessive pot smoking wasn't just a habit—it was a form of escapism. She tried everything to get him to stop, from pleading to ultimatums, but nothing worked. Her constant efforts to control his behavior only added strain to their marriage.

It wasn't until her husband left in a rage and didn't return for a week that Ruth finally sought support. A neighbor suggested she attend a recovery program for families of addicts. At her first meeting, Ruth was shocked to find people who seemed genuinely happy, even though their loved ones were battling addiction. That night, she learned a critical truth: *She didn't cause her husband's addiction, and in no way could she stop it.*

By focusing on herself instead of her husband's choices, Ruth began to reclaim her life. She practiced self-care, reconnected with her passions, and stopped trying to control what was out of her hands. This shift didn't make her husband's behavior any easier to deal with, but it gave Ruth the strength and clarity to approach the situation from a healthier place.

WHEN YOU WORRY OBSESSIVELY

When fear takes the driver's seat in our lives, it engulfs us in worry. We become fixated on worst-case scenarios, unable to see reality clearly. Compassion and empathy fall by the wayside, replaced by self-centered-ness and a constant loop of anxiety. This behavior is the antithesis of *Living Richly*—it keeps us stuck, disconnected from others, and detached from our true power.

Take Geralyn, for example. She was an incessant worrier, fed up with how her life had turned out. Geralyn's mother was a worrier, and so was her grandmother. The habit had been passed down like an heirloom. By her forties, Geralyn was living alone, working as an elementary school teacher, and spending her evenings watching television or obsessing over the news. One Saturday night, feeling deeply depressed and comparing her life to others, she closed her eyes and thought, *"My life isn't going anywhere."*

That moment sparked a shift. She remembered a minister at her church talking about a vision board—assembling images of what you want your life to look like. Skeptical but desperate, she grabbed a pad from her desk and started to draw. She sketched herself with a partner and a young child, a life filled with connection and joy. Geralyn realized she couldn't make it happen alone. She resolved to reach out to the minister for guidance the following Sunday.

This was Geralyn's first step toward letting go of her false self, the part of her that dwelled on worry. By trusting her intuition, she began to reclaim her power.

UNDERSTANDING YOUR POWER

Power isn't about controlling others or dominating a situation. True power is multidimensional. It includes compassion, the ability to confront, and knowing when to remain silent. These dimensions of power allow us to act authentically rather than react out of fear or insecurity.

COMPASSIONATE POWER

Compassionate power is the ability to listen deeply—not just to words but to moods, body language, and what's left unsaid. It requires focus and a quieting of your own Mad Mind-Chatter. When you use compassionate power, the other person feels heard, which fosters connection and trust.

Nancy embodied compassionate power. A former nurse who transitioned to a career in finance, she brought her empathy and ability to connect to her interactions with people. No matter how busy she was, Nancy always took the time to ask how you were doing, and her interest felt genuine.

I remember sharing a challenge I was having with my son. Nancy listened without judgment, shared her own similar experience, and offered thoughtful, actionable feedback. Her calming presence and genuine concern made her a trusted friend and colleague.

CONFRONTATIVE POWER

Sometimes, acting authentically means standing up and speaking out. Integrity is the barometer for confrontative power—it's about addressing what is wrong, false, or unjust. Remaining silent in these moments is a form of complicity.

Stacy was known among her friends for her directness. If someone behaved rudely or unfairly, she would call it out. She wasn't aggressive or brash, but her honesty made her a reliable ally when accountability was needed. Her friends depended on her to pinpoint issues and address them confidently.

SILENT POWER

Silence is often underestimated as a form of power. A well-timed pause or refusal to engage can communicate more than words ever could. Silence creates space for reflection and often compels others to take notice of or reconsider their own actions.

Rusty was a master of silent power. Reflective and spiritual, her presence was magnetic. People often sought her advice, knowing her words would be thoughtful and precise. If Rusty disagreed with something, she didn't feel the need to explain or defend her position. A simple, *"Not how I see it,"* was enough. Her brevity carried weight, making her opinions respected and valued.

KNOWING WHICH POWER TO USE

Different situations call for different approaches. Here are some examples to illustrate when to use compassionate, confrontative, or silent power.

- **Scenario 1:** You're sitting with your boss, who has outlined a business strategy you disagree with. He hasn't asked for your opinion and has made it clear he's taking the lead at the meeting. In this case, use silent power. Allow your actions and contributions to speak for themselves when the time is right.
- **Scenario 2:** Your mother-in-law complains that she hasn't seen her grandchildren in over a month, implying neglect on your part. Rather than reacting defensively, use compassionate power. Acknowledge her feelings and show understanding: *"I know it's been a while, and I can see how much you miss them. Let's figure out a time to get together soon."*
- **Scenario 3:** At a school meeting, the principal announces that part of the music program will be eliminated to prioritize a sporting event. Your child and others cherish being part of the chorus, which is now at risk. Here, confrontative power is necessary. Speak up calmly and assertively: *"I understand the importance of athletics, but the chorus provides incredible value to our children. Is there a way to reconsider this decision?"*

TAKE YOUR POWER BACK

Letting go of our false selves allows us to act authentically. Whether through compassion, confrontation, or silence, we begin to show up in meaningful ways. Like Geralyn, we can move beyond worry and into action. Like Nancy, we can connect with empathy. Like Stacy, we can stand up for what's right. And like Rusty, we can embrace the quiet strength of being fully present.

Living Richly Practice:
Coming from Power

There's a profound difference between *acting* and *reacting*. When something stressful happens, our first instinct is often to react— reverting to old patterns of behavior that may have protected us in the past. These knee-jerk reactions bypass reflection, and while they may offer a temporary sense of control, they rarely lead to the best outcomes.

To avoid being impulsive, we need to pause before we act. The next time you're confronted with an unexpected situation, take a moment. Breathe deeply. Reflect on what's happening and what the best course of action might be. Then, act from your power—not from fear or habit.

This shift isn't easy. Old behaviors can feel ingrained, and breaking free from them can feel like standing in a hallway—neither where you were nor where you're going. It's uncomfortable, uncertain, and often unsettling. I've been in that hallway many times, and what has gotten me through is faith. Trusting that something better is on the horizon, even when I can't see it, has carried me forward.

Growth comes when we lean into that discomfort. Bearing the uncertainty of change can lead to some of the most transformative moments in our lives. In the next chapter, we'll explore how to put fear into its proper perspective so it no longer paralyzes us or leads to inaction.

EXPANDED CHAPTER TAKEAWAYS

Being joyful takes work.

to popular belief, joy doesn't just happen — it often requires both effort and intentionality. *Living Richly* means being vigilant about what can steal your happiness. This includes being aware of your Mad Mind-Chatter, the constant stream of negativity and self-doubt that plays in your head. When you notice these thoughts, the challenge is consciously changing the channel to something more positive and empowering.

Certain habits detract from our power.

Behaviors like the need to be right, doing everything yourself, trying to control others, or worrying incessantly may feel familiar, even comforting in the moment. Still, they ultimately rob us of our ability to act authentically. These habits create tension in our relationships and distract us from what truly matters. Letting go of these tendencies isn't easy, but it's necessary to reclaim your energy and focus on living a more meaningful life.

Authenticity is the foundation of joy.

To live richly, you must be authentic—connect with your true self and act in alignment with your values. This means letting go of the masks we wear to gain approval or avoid conflict. When you act authentically, you stop betraying yourself and build relationships based on mutual respect and understanding.

Power is multidimensional.

True power isn't about control or dominance. It's about showing up in each moment with compassion, integrity, and presence. Power can take different forms:

- **Compassionate power** is listening deeply and connecting with others on an emotional level.
- **Confrontative power** is standing up for what's right and addressing issues directly but with integrity.
- **Silent power** is knowing when to hold your tongue, creating space for others to reflect and reconsider.

Each form of power has its place, and learning when to use it is key to navigating life's challenges with grace and confidence.

NUGGET FROM THE HEART

When you drop the act, you'll realize you've *always* had the power to live a rich, expansive life.

FOR YOUR JOURNAL

1. Reflect on a time when you cared too much about someone else's opinion and reacted dishonestly. What happened as a result? Now, imagine how the situation might have unfolded if you had responded honestly and authentically.
2. Think about a time recently when you used compassionate power. How did it feel to genuinely connect with someone? What impact did it have on the relationship?

CHAPTER 3

LETTING GO OF PARALYZING FEAR

Fear loses its power when you face it, understand it, and move through it.

Fear has a way of stopping us in our tracks, keeping us stuck in cycles of doubt and inaction. We've discussed how fear can prevent us from *Living Richly*, but now it's time to explore how to loosen its grip.

Fear isn't always a villain—it can serve a purpose. Sometimes, it alerts us to real danger or helps us prepare for a challenging situation. Other times, excitement can disguise itself as fear, creating a mix of emotions we misinterpret. The problem arises when fear is misused—when we let imagined scenarios take over our thoughts, paralyzing us with worry about outcomes that never come to pass.

To move past fear, we must understand the situations that evoke it, recognize it for what it is, and reframe our thoughts to move forward. Let's start with some examples of common fears and how they can be reframed.

FACING AND REFRAMING COMMON FEARS

Do any of these sound familiar?

Negative thought: *"I resent people who are living a great life! I'll never be like them."*

These thoughts often hide a fear of putting yourself out there and failing. It is easier to resent others than to take a risk.

> **Reframing:** *"Yes, I could fail, but I could also succeed. I'll never know unless I try, and I won't give up."*

Negative thought: *"I've tried so many times to get that _____, but nothing materializes. Why bother!"*

Underlying this statement is disappointment and the fear of failing.

> **Reframing:** *"Each time I try, I learn something new. Every attempt brings me closer to success.*

Negative thought: *"If I were smarter, prettier, wealthier, or more talented, I'd succeed, and things would be different."*

Here, the fear of failing provides an excuse like the other examples that keep us from acting.

> **Reframing:** *"This kind of thinking paralyzes me. I don't need to wait to be different—I can take a small step toward getting what I want right now."*

THE ROLE OF DESTRUCTIVE HABITS

Fear doesn't just show up in obvious ways; it hides in destructive habits like perfectionism, second-guessing, and procrastination. These habits may feel protective, but they reinforce fear, keeping us stuck.

Perfectionism

Perfectionism is the fear of imperfection dressed up as diligence. It's a constant worry that what you're doing isn't good enough. Perfectionists spend endless hours fine-tuning small details, rarely feeling satisfied with their work. They micromanage, anticipate worst-case scenarios, and hold themselves to impossible standards, often ignoring their accomplishments or the achievements of others.

This mindset creates an imaginary straitjacket, leading to feelings of inadequacy and exhaustion. It's a cycle that takes a toll on self-esteem, relationships, and joy.

Strategies for Overcoming Perfectionism

Breaking free from perfectionism means learning to trust your abilities. Positive self-talk is key. Say to yourself, *"Everything will get done. Maybe not perfectly, but that is okay."*

Also, when you complete a task, take a moment to acknowledge your accomplishment before diving into the next one. Reflect on what you've done well instead of focusing on what you could have done better.

Mistakes are inevitable, but they're also opportunities to learn. Instead of agonizing over them, treat them as stepping stones for growth. Then, move on with confidence.

BEATRICE'S STORY

Beatrice, a real estate agent, had a recent experience that highlighted the need to let go of perfectionism. She had been working on getting an important listing for weeks, pouring her time and energy into it. In a highly competitive market, she put forth a conservative price to the seller of what she thought the property would sell for, hoping to leave room for negotiation with her prospective client. However, her competitor immediately presented a higher price, and the client chose them.

At first, Beatrice was consumed by regret. She replayed the situation in her mind, criticizing herself for losing the listing. Her daughter saw her frustration and encouraged her to forgive herself. That evening, they attended their weekly dance class. Beatrice was able to laugh and have some fun.

In hindsight, Beatrice learned a valuable lesson about her market—next time, she'll immediately give the seller a range of prices from high to low. Her daughter's support reminded her that life is about more than one setback.

Embracing Fear with Courage

Letting go of fear doesn't mean eliminating it entirely; it means facing it with courage. Each time fear arises, it offers a choice: stay stuck in old patterns or move forward with resilience.

The next time fear tells you to stop, ask yourself: *What's the worst that could happen?* Often, the answer is far less daunting than the fear itself. Then, remind yourself: *What's the best thing that could happen?* Focus on that possibility and take the next step.

As you learn to reframe fear and its related habits, you'll find that *Living Richly* is not about avoiding failure but about embracing the lessons that come with it.

Living Richly Practice
Life Is Messy

Life isn't about perfection; it's about recognizing the beauty in imperfection, the joy in spontaneity, and the lessons in the chaos. Here's a simple exercise to connect with that messy, creative part of yourself:

Purchase some finger paints, lay out a piece of paper, and put on music that inspires you. Give yourself twenty minutes to paint. Don't worry about how it looks. Just let your hands move, let the colors blend, and enjoy the process. Your picture won't be perfect, but there's joy in letting go and embracing the messiness of life.

SECOND-GUESSING YOURSELF

Have you ever made a well-thought-out decision only to doubt yourself afterward? It's as though fear creeps in to undo all your hard work and clarity. I know this pattern all too well, and so did Sybil.

Sybil owned a successful marketing company, which she decided to sell so she could spend more time with her young granddaughter and finally travel. She carefully consulted a coach and thought through every aspect of her decision. Yet, after the deal went through, she began to second-guess herself. The business was doing exceptionally well for its new owners, and she couldn't help but wonder if she had sold too soon. *"Should I have held on for another year?"* she agonized.

This kind of thinking only agitated Sybil further. Eventually, she realized how much unnecessary stress she was causing herself. In her words: *"The deal is done, and I need to focus on what truly matters. This was the right time in my life to make this move. Money wasn't the only factor—my priorities now are time with my family and exploring the world."*

Remember Sybil's lesson when self-doubt arises: trust your decision and redirect your focus to the opportunities ahead.

Living Richly **Practice**
Get On with It!

If you find yourself doubting a decision you've already made, say *"No!"* out loud to the negative thoughts. Then, redirect your energy— call a friend, but don't discuss the decision. Instead, talk about something that brings you joy. Distraction and affirmation are powerful tools to break the cycle of second-guessing.

OVERCOMING PROCRASTINATION

Procrastination is often rooted in fear of failure, rejection, or not being good enough. The irony is that delaying action only adds to anxiety and stress. Paulette's story is a perfect example.

Paulette had been a bank teller for two years. She aspired to become a supervisor but kept postponing the conversation with her boss. She feared he wouldn't see her leadership potential, and that fear paralyzed her. As a result, her procrastination began affecting her performance. She felt distracted, and even simple tasks took longer than usual.

One night over dinner, her mother gave her a much-needed pep talk: *"Paulette, they need smart young women like you. If you don't ask for it, you'll never get it."* Those words gave Paulette the courage to schedule a meeting with her boss. Taking that first step was liberating, and she realized the opportunity had been waiting for her all along—she just needed to claim it.

STRATEGY FOR OVERCOMING PROCRASTINATION

The key to conquering procrastination is making a start, no matter how small. Take a single step toward your goal and acknowledge your progress. Create a checklist with a clear timetable for each action. If you struggle to stay accountable, enlist the help of a trusted friend to keep you on track. Momentum builds with action, and soon, fear will lose its hold.

Living Richly **Practice**
Trace the Fear

When you're avoiding a task, ask yourself: *What am I afraid of?* Write down the negative thoughts and fears running through your mind. How would you feel if you continued to delay? Let the discomfort of procrastination motivate you to take a small action toward completing the task.

REFRAMING FEAR THROUGH SERVICE

What keeps me moving forward despite my fears is my desire to be of service. When I shift my focus from myself to how I can help others, fear fades into the background. Here's how this works in practice:

At a conference, surrounded by strangers, fear might whisper: *"You don't know anyone here. This is overwhelming."*

Reframing it through service sounds like: *"Let me find someone who looks nervous and offer them a smile or start a conversation."*

Before a job interview, fear might say, *"You're not qualified enough for this position."*

Reframing it through service looks like this: *"I have valuable skills to offer this company, and I'll focus on communicating them clearly."*

On a blind date, fear might shout: *"Your track record in relationships is terrible—this will end badly."*

Reframing it through service sounds like: *"I'll focus on getting to know this person and being open about who I am. That's all I need to do."*

When we approach situations with the intention to serve others, we quiet our fears and step into the present moment.

Take this example:

A woman who's feeling depressed about her failing relationship, afraid of being alone, walks out of her building, and she sees a child dart into the street. He is unaware of an oncoming car. Without hesitation, the woman rushes to pull the child to safety.

In that moment, fear disappears. Her focus shifts entirely to the immediate need—to be of service. This connection to others is the antidote to isolation, which fear often creates.

THE CONNECTION BETWEEN FEAR AND EXCITEMENT

Did you know that fear and excitement create the same physical reactions in the body? Your heart races, your palms sweat, and butterflies flutter in your stomach. The difference lies in how you interpret those sensations.

When preparing for a big event—whether a television appearance or a speaking engagement—I feel the rush of adrenaline and think, *"I must be nervous."* But when I pause and examine those feelings, I often realize I'm excited. Shifting my perspective allows me to focus on the positive aspects of the situation rather than dwelling on fear.

The next time you step out of your comfort zone, don't be so quick to label your feelings as fear. Consider that what you're experiencing might be excitement—a sign that something thrilling is about to happen.

Living Richly Practice
Do a Double Take

When you feel fear creeping in as you consider stepping into something new, pause and take a closer look—do a double take. Is it truly fear, or is it excitement in disguise? You might be surprised by the answer. If it's excitement, use that energy to anticipate the best.

Imagine the possibilities, the opportunities, and the growth that could come from stepping outside your comfort zone. This was true for Lillie, who found a renewed sense of purpose after brain surgery. During her recovery, her fears could have easily consumed her, leaving her isolated and discouraged. Instead, her family encouraged her to write—a passion she hadn't indulged in for years. Lillie joined a Zoom writing group and began creating short stories. To her delight, writing brought Lillie immense joy and became a source of healing and self-expression.

When you reframe fear as excitement, you open yourself to new ideas, projects, and connections.

FANTASIZE AND CHANGE THE CHANNEL

Imagine it's Monday morning, and instead of dreading the start of the week, you approach it differently. Picture yourself incorporating a fun activity into your day: a walk in the park, a coffee date with a friend, or trying something entirely new.

Even small shifts in your routine can expand your ability to live richly and see life from a new perspective.

Luna's story is a powerful example of this. Born in Manhattan, her parents immigrated from Spain. Luna found herself in her 50s at a crossroads. She was about to retire from her government job, divorced, and living alone. When her uncle left her a small house outside Barcelona, she planned to visit, fix it up, and sell it. Fear, however, kept her from considering living there. Starting over seemed too overwhelming.

But when Luna finally visited the house, she fell in love with the area. The warmth of the community, the charm of the home, and the opportunity to work at a nearby craft shop made her reconsider. When she returned to Manhattan, it no longer felt like home. A few months later, Luna decided to give herself three months in Spain as a trial run. The experience was transformative. She found joy, friendship, and purpose in ways she hadn't anticipated.

Living expansively, as Luna discovered, often requires moving through fear and embracing change. However, with new routines and opportunities, time management can become a challenge. That's where time-tracking tools come in handy.

Living Richly **Practice**
Create a Daily Time Plan

Managing your time doesn't have to be complicated. A simple daily plan can help you prioritize activities and keep track of what you've accomplished. You can combine work and personal tasks or you can separate them and have two time sheets. Here is an example of a time sheet:

Time	Activity
7:00 AM	Meditate, Prayer Practice
7:30 AM	Swim
8:05 AM	Quick Breakfast with Kids
8:30 AM	Travel to Work
9:15 AM	Meet with Web Editor
10:00 AM	Pitch to Susan B
11:00 AM	Call Leads
12:30 PM	Haircut
1:30 PM	Quick Lunch
2:05 PM	Meet with Team
3:00 PM	Pitch to Jack R
4:00 PM	Research Projects
5:30 PM	Travel Home
7:00 PM	Dinner with Family
8:15 PM	Relax (Read, Watch TV)
11:00 PM	Bedtime

This structure helps you stay on track with work priorities while leaving space for relaxation and connection with loved ones. The goal isn't perfection—it's progress.

REKINDLING RELATIONSHIPS

As you move through fear and into a richer way of living, the value of your relationships becomes even more apparent. They are the spice of life. Spending time with loved ones is priceless, yet it's easy to let important connections fall by the wayside.

Luna's story reminds us of the importance of community. For her, rekindling relationships in a new environment brought joy and a renewed sense of belonging. For you, it might mean reaching out to a family member, an old friend, or a former colleague.

Don't let the opportunity to reconnect slip away. Today, reach out to someone you've lost touch with. A phone call, a handwritten note, or even a simple text can remind you of your connection. Life is unpredictable, and the opportunity to reconnect may not always be there.

WHEN FEAR MASQUERADES AS SERIOUSNESS

Fear can be a master of disguise. One of its favorite costumes? Seriousness. Sometimes, when stepping out of our comfort zone feels overwhelming, we may respond by taking ourselves too seriously. This seriousness can drain joy and laughter from our lives, leaving us more entrenched in fear.

Are you laughing enough? If not, it's time to add more fun to your life. Fun has the power to lighten our fears, give us new perspectives, and refresh our minds. Laughter and play free us to approach even the most ordinary situations with renewed energy and enthusiasm.

Imagine this: You come home from work, exhausted and overwhelmed by worry. All you want to do is collapse into bed. Then, a good friend calls. She's full of jokes, and her laughter is infectious. Suddenly, your mood shifts. You feel lighter, free! So much so that you'd rather meet her for dinner than go to sleep.

THE WONDER OF PLAY

Play isn't just for children; it's a lifeline for adults, too. When we allow ourselves to laugh, dance, or engage in something whimsical, we create space for joy, no matter what our challenges are. Danielle, for example, learned this lesson in an unexpected way.

Danielle loved Bon Bons—those chocolate-covered ice cream treats—as a child. She came up with the idea of "spiritual Bon Bons" and carried it into adulthood, using it as a way to seek reassurance. One day, she found herself worried about her neighborhood after the local recreation center was torn down. Walking home from work, she sent out her plea: *"Ok, God, please send me a spiritual Bon Bon!"*

As she approached the site of the former center, she heard music. A man with a banjo had gathered a small crowd on the sidewalk, inviting people to join him in singing. Danielle felt her worry melt away as she joined the group. At that moment, she realized there would be a solution to the neighborhood's challenge, even if she did not know what it was.

Living Richly Practice
RX for Intimidation

Laughter has the power to dissolve fear. Before meeting someone who intimidates you, try this exercise: Picture that person doing something utterly ridiculous—like chasing a mouse around the room or wearing mismatched socks to an important meeting. The mental image will lighten your mood and help you approach the interaction with greater ease.

LOOKING AHEAD

Moving through our fears, we invite more joy into our lives. The next Key in our *Living Richly* program is learning how to open ourselves up to receiving abundance. Chapter Four will show you how to embrace what's coming your way.

CHAPTER TAKEAWAYS

- Fear doesn't have to stop you. You can be afraid and still take meaningful action.
- Perfectionism, second-guessing yourself, and procrastination are habits that keep you stuck, but with practice, you can break free.
- When you approach life with a spirit of service, you'll discover that helping others dissolves fear.
- Recognize the fine line between fear and excitement, opt for a positive outcome, and don't forget the magic of "spiritual Bon Bons"—those little signs and moments of joy that remind you everything will be okay.

NUGGET FROM THE HEART

Don't let fear stop you when you know you can make an impact.

FOR YOUR JOURNAL

1 Describe an incident in the last year when you were afraid but also excited about trying something new.

2. Do you take yourself too seriously? If so, why do you think that is? Go deeper. What are you afraid of?

3. Keep track of your time this week. What activities would you like more time for? What activities are taking up too much of your time that you could eliminate?

THE SECOND KEY

GETTING MORE

A prosperous life is within your reach—believe, and you will receive.

CHAPTER 4

❧

BEING OPEN TO RECEIVING

Whoever you are, whatever you do—it's time to let the "good stuff" in.

*I*n the First Key, **Giving Up**, we explored the importance of releasing habits that no longer serve you, especially the feeling of being a victim. *Living Richly* and feeling deprived can't coexist. It's a tall order, but I know you're up for the challenge. Now, you're ready for the Second Key: **Getting More** of the "good stuff." This is about receiving abundance in every area of your life: family, friendships, career, and more. The secret? Learning how to let it in.

As women, far too many of us struggle to accept what we secretly crave: admiration, acknowledgment, awards, money, and promotions. We're making progress, yes—but it's still a challenge. Why? Because giving has been ingrained in us from a young age.

Think about it. As girls, we're taught to be "nice," to think of others first, to stay in the background, and to avoid the spotlight. We carry this conditioning into adulthood, where we're relied on for everything—as mothers, workers, daughters, and caregivers. Giving becomes second nature. Receiving? That's where things get uncomfortable.

THE STRUGGLE TO RECEIVE

I know this struggle well. I've lived it. One moment stands out clearly in my mind, a moment that should have been a celebration but instead highlighted my discomfort with receiving.

I was on stage in front of hundreds of people, accepting an Emmy for my public television show, *Proud to Be a Girl*. I smiled and thanked the audience, but I felt uncomfortable inside. I couldn't wait to leave the podium.

When I returned to my table, people congratulated me: *"Way to go, great job, Helene!"* Instead of basking in their praise, I felt really awkward.

Why couldn't I just *accept* their kind words? Why did the act of receiving make me feel so vulnerable?

Here's what I realized: When we're giving, we're in control. We're initiating the action. But when we're receiving, we relinquish that control. Even when the "good stuff" is offered—admiration, acknowledgment, or rewards—it can feel foreign or undeserved. Receiving stirred up a more profound question: Why didn't I feel worthy of it?

THE WEIGHT OF THE IMPOSTER SYNDROME

At that moment, I didn't feel like I belonged on that stage. I felt like an imposter. Sure, I created a powerful television program, managed a large team, and handled a significant production budget. But doubts nagged at me: *Did I really deserve this recognition?*

It was madness. I poured my passion into the documentary, learned quickly, and sought advice from trusted mentors along the way. Yes, there were mistakes, but there were also countless successes.

With the First Key, we focused on letting go of what I call Mad Mind-Chatter. This inner dialogue can be relentless, like calling me an imposter. I wasn't alone in this experience. You've likely heard of imposter syndrome

—the persistent feeling of being a fraud, even in the face of accomplishments. It's often associated with women, but I've learned it's not exclusive to us.

During a virtual event in the height of Covid, a male participant admitted he felt like an imposter. "My wife has all the confidence in the family," he joked. His honesty was refreshing and a reminder that this struggle may not be gender-specific.

The key to overcoming it is awareness and challenging its validity. The moment you notice a negative thought, ask yourself, "Is this true?" If it's not based on reality, redirect your focus to something productive.

WHY RECEIVING MATTERS

If you can't receive, you're cutting yourself off from abundance. Whether it's an opportunity, a compliment, or support from someone who believes in you, receiving is the gateway to growth.

But here's the good news: learning to receive is a skill, and like any skill, it gets easier with practice.

Living Richly Practice
Receiving a Compliment

Take a moment to think about the last time someone gave you a compliment or an acknowledgment. Did you brush it off? Deflect it? Say something like, *"Oh, it's nothing"*?

Next time, stop yourself. Look the person in the eye and say, *"Thank you."* Let their words sink in. Feel the warmth of their admiration.

Every time you practice receiving, you strengthen your ability to let prosperity flow into your life.

COMMON DISTRACTIONS THAT KEEP YOU FROM RECEIVING

Living Richly is about managing distractions and focusing your energy on achieving what you truly want. While distractions will inevitably arise, you are in charge of what you let in.

Do any of these resonate with you?

- **Focusing on others instead of yourself.** I've learned the value of minding my own business.
- **Having a closed mind.** This mindset keeps you small, stuck in a poverty mentality.
- **Dwelling on problems.** Obsessing over challenges creates despair and zaps your hope.
- **Feeling guilty.** Guilt serves no purpose beyond draining your energy and keeping you from joy.

Self-care often triggers guilt, especially when you feel like you should be prioritizing others—children, elders, and work responsibilities. But let's reframe the way we look at self-care: It's not selfish; it's essential. Taking time for yourself is an act of self-love, a way of replenishing your energy so you can give from a full cup.

TRUSTING YOURSELF TO RECEIVE

Receiving is an act of trust. It's about taking in what you need and letting go of what you don't. This trust comes from knowing your track record—recognizing the times you've made good decisions despite doubts. And when you feel uncertain, it helps to have faith in something greater than yourself.

For me, this faith has been a constant companion, even from a young age. I remember walking down a country road as a child, feeling the sun on my face and hearing the birds chirping. In that moment, I felt part of something vast and beautiful, far beyond my understanding. That presence stayed with me through my teenage years, but it wasn't until my twenties that my faith truly deepened.

A TURNING POINT

As I mentioned, in my early twenties I was at a breaking point. I had gained a lot of weight and felt hopeless after trying countless diets that didn't work. The only way out seemed like ending my life. But deep within me, I heard a voice shout, *"No, there is more for you to do."* [*]

That voice was so forceful, I couldn't ignore it. It guided me to a support group that not only helped me lose weight but also introduced me to a new way of living. Trusting that voice—and the process it led me to—was frightening. I had no proof that it would work, but the reassurance and encouragement from the group gave me the strength to believe that it could.

FAITH IN THE RICHNESS OF LIFE

Today, I have an unshakable faith in my higher self, that part of me that supports my well-being and comforts me in challenging times. This faith allows me to take bold actions and *Live Richly* without letting fear run the show.

I invite you to embrace this perspective: Trust that something greater than your mind-talk (your higher self, God, or universal goodness) is on your side. Trusting in something greater than your incessant thoughts doesn't mean abandoning responsibility; it means partnering with a force that supports your well-being. Assume its guidance is always available to you and take action toward your goals until you are shown otherwise.

[*] Helene Lerner, *In Her Power: Reclaiming Your Authentic Self* (Oregon: Beyond Words, New York: Atria, 2012), x.

TAKE REASONABLE ACTIONS UNTIL SHOWN DIFFERENTLY

While we can't control everything, we can take small steps forward with faith, knowing that clarity will come in time. It's a balance between action and patience. Sylvia's story illustrates how trust can lead to solutions that expand your life in ways you never imagined.

Sylvia's life was deeply intertwined with her granddaughter, Mary. As a single father, Sylvia's son Jack relied on her to help care for Mary after school. Sylvia was devastated when Jack announced he was relocating from New York City to San Francisco for a career opportunity. Over dinner, Jack explained how his company would cover all relocation expenses and that the role was too important to pass up. Overwhelmed with emotion, Sylvia couldn't imagine life without seeing Mary every day. "Jack, I have to think about this. You're asking me to relocate and leave my life here," she said tearfully. "I had no idea this was happening."

That night, Sylvia turned to prayer, seeking guidance on what to do. The following day, she reached out to friends at her church. One friend suggested a compromise: Jack could help cover her expenses so she could keep her New York apartment. Sylvia could live with Jack and Mary during the winter and return to New York in the summer. The idea gave her a sense of comfort. Inspired, Sylvia called Jack and shared the suggestion. He was immediately on board, happy to find a solution that worked for everyone.

Sylvia's willingness to trust in the process allowed her to receive the guidance she needed. She didn't resist or dwell on the challenge; instead, she took reasonable steps by reaching out for support and remaining open to creative solutions. What could have been a heartbreaking situation transformed into an opportunity. Sylvia not only maintained her bond with Mary but also expanded her world. She gained the chance to spend time on both coasts, form new relationships in California, and keep her roots in New York City.

Trusting doesn't mean surrendering control entirely. It's about acting with faith that the next right action will reveal itself. Sylvia didn't know the exact outcome when she first prayed for guidance, but her openness allowed her to receive the answers she needed.

When challenges arise, trust can guide you through uncertainty. Take reasonable actions, seek advice, explore possibilities, and remain open to help. Solutions often come when you're willing to move forward, even when the path isn't entirely clear.

Living Richly Practice
Allowing Yourself to Receive the "Good Stuff"

Imagine yourself at a vibrant country fair, filled with vendors offering their finest products, delicious food stands, and exciting amusement rides. Now, picture this: everything at the fair is completely free for the next fifteen minutes. There's no catch, no limit, and no strings attached.

How do you respond?

Do you grab a small bag and carefully pick a few items, telling yourself not to take too much so others can have their share? Or do you confidently gather several large shopping bags, trusting that there's more than enough for everyone, including you?

This scenario reflects how open—or closed—you are to *Living Richly*. The truth is, there is more than enough for everyone, and when we embrace this truth, our lives expand in ways we never thought possible.

SHIFTING FROM LIMITATION TO EXPANSION

Living Richly means moving beyond scarcity and embracing a prosperity mindset. It's not just about material wealth; it's also about the richness of experiences, opportunities, and relationships. The key is learning to receive.

THE POWER OF RECEIVING

Imagine your life as a funnel. When you try to control everything, the funnel narrows. Opportunities, joy, and abundance struggle to flow in. But the funnel widens when you trust and allow yourself to receive freely. Suddenly, there's more room for possibility, growth, and wealth.

We must shift our mindset from *"there is not enough abundance for everyone"* to *"there is more than enough for all of us."*

WALKING ON THE BRIGHT SIDE

Life is infinitely more joyful when we envision positive outcomes rather than letting fear and doubt dictate our actions. We have a choice to receive or try to control situations, which influences the richness of our experiences. Let's look at these examples:

A friend unexpectedly treats you to a movie. If you're open to receiving, you might hug her and express your gratitude, savoring the generosity of the gesture. But if you're trying to control the situation, your mind might immediately jump to *"How can I reciprocate? I must give back something of equal value as soon as possible."* Instead of appreciating the moment, you're consumed by obligation, missing the joy of the connection.

Or consider a long-lost sister visiting after years abroad. If you can receive the reunion openly, you might think, *"I'm excited to see her. Sure, we had our differences as teenagers, but I have such fond memories of our childhood. I'm looking forward to catching up!"* Contrast that with trying to control the outcome: *"We fought a lot before she left, and we'll probably start fighting again. I've arranged to meet my friend Carla if things go south.* Fear and doubt drive this narrative, keeping you from being fully present and open to the possibility of a joyful reunion.

These scenarios highlight a simple truth: We allow space for joy and connection when we trust and let go. But when we try to control ourselves, fear and doubt rob us of those opportunities.

BUILDING SELF-TRUST

Trusting yourself is foundational to *Living Richly*. It's about recalling your past successes, acknowledging your resilience, and believing in your ability to navigate life's uncertainties. When trust feels elusive, additional support can help.

Living Richly Practice
Filling Your Self-Trust Wallet

This practice is designed to strengthen your trust in yourself, even when you don't yet have proof that what you desire will manifest. It requires discipline, awareness, and the support of a like-minded partner.

1. Start a Self-Trust Wallet: This can be a notebook, a digital document, or a physical wallet where you keep notes about moments you trusted yourself and succeeded. Write down times, big or small, when you made a decision, took a step forward, and saw positive results.

2. Set a Goal: Identify an area where you want to build self-trust, such as relationships, your career, or your health.

3. Daily Awareness: Throughout the day, notice when you've taken action in this area. When you succeed, write a note about your win and put it in your wallet.

4. Get a Trust Buddy: Find someone who also wants to build trust in themselves. Set up a weekly meeting to read your notes, celebrate your wins, and encourage each other when you fall short. This mutual accountability helps reinforce the practice and provides support when self-doubt arises. Also, listen to their feedback and use their constructive input to grow and improve.

THE COURAGE TO RECEIVE AND GIVE FEEDBACK

Feedback, especially the kind that challenges us, can feel like a gut punch. But when delivered sincerely, it has the power to reshape our lives. The key is learning how to accept it without defensiveness.

Most people tend to take feedback personally, but growth requires us to pause, breathe, and process before reacting. When feedback comes from someone who cares, it's meant for our development. Take what serves you and discard the rest.

In my own life, the most painful feedback has led to my most significant breakthroughs. When someone was brave enough to tell me what I didn't want to hear, I discovered truths about myself that fueled my growth. This principle applies in every area of life—from work to personal relationships.

Let me share the stories of four remarkable women who embraced feedback and transformed their lives.

SUSAN'S LEAP INTO VISIBILITY

Susan, a coach in her mid-40s, was stuck in a cycle of frustration. She dreamed of creating online courses but was paralyzed by fear. As we dug deeper, we uncovered the roots of her self-doubt: a childhood filled with criticism from her grandmother, who raised her. Her fear of stepping into the spotlight wasn't just about the present; it was an echo of her past.

I helped Susan reframe her mindset and take actionable steps toward her dream. Over time, she silenced the negative voices in her head and launched her online courses. Today, Susan is thriving, reaching thousands of people with her message. Her courage to face feedback changed her destiny.

ROSALYN'S TRIP OF A LIFETIME

Rosalyn's story is one of resilience. Diagnosed with breast cancer, now in remission, she faced her health challenges head-on and decided to retire early. But fear crept in—fear of spending her savings and leaving her financial comfort zone.

When her spouse suggested a dream trip to Tahiti, Rosalyn hesitated. "You've wanted this for years," her partner said. "Let's live now!" After many sleepless nights, she said yes. The transformative trip reminded her that life is about experiences, not just security. Rosalyn is now living a fulfilling life, one courageous decision at a time.

KAREN'S BREAKTHROUGH IN ACTING

Karen, an aspiring actress, was stuck in disappointment. She attended auditions but wasn't getting callbacks. In a moment of vulnerability, she shared her struggles with a group of actors, and their feedback was clear: "Feel the disappointment, but don't let it stop you. Keep going!"

The next day, Karen faced yet another rejection but refused to spiral into negativity. Instead, she took action, made calls and put herself out there. Her persistence paid off when she landed a role as a regular on a local TV show, earning ten times more than the opportunity she had initially pursued. Feedback from her peers gave her the push she needed to achieve a great job.

ANDREA'S SHIFT FROM BLAME

Andrea, a woman with grown children and a struggling marriage, came to me feeling stuck. She owned a flower shop that was barely breaking even and spent much of her energy criticizing her husband. I told her the truth she needed to hear: that her hypercritical mindset was draining her and sabotaging her success. At first, she resisted, but eventually, she realized her approach wasn't working. She became willing to try something different.

I challenged Andrea to reflect on what bothered her most about her husband. She admitted he wasn't aggressively pursuing opportunities, mirroring her own reluctance in business. The real transformation began when she shifted her focus inward. She stopped complaining (using a wristband as a reminder) and doubled her sales calls. Within weeks, her husband surprised her with a romantic dinner, and a prestigious client entered her shop. Andrea's willingness to listen and act on my feedback unlocked the doors to her success.

Living Richly Practice
Embrace the Gift of Feedback

Feedback isn't just information; it's a disguised gift, often wrapped in a challenge. When you receive feedback, repeat it to the person to show you've understood. This simple act creates space for reflection and diffuses defensiveness. For example, after a performance review, you might say, "You're pleased with most of my work, but I've made mistakes on the client's report and need to proofread more carefully." Or to your teenager, "You're upset because I missed your last two soccer games, and you need me to be there for the next one."

By restating what has been said, you create a moment of calm to process the feedback. Then, let the other person know you'll think about their comments and follow up (set a specific time). This practice allows you to engage with feedback thoughtfully rather than react impulsively.

NAVIGATING THE UPS AND DOWNS OF CHANGE

Receiving feedback can be challenging, and adapting to it is even tougher. Some days, it will feel like everything is aligning perfectly. Other days, you'll be holding on tight, overwhelmed by emotions, doubts, or challenges. Both are part of the process.

Be kind to yourself. Changing your habits or mindset takes time—not just for you but also for those around you who might still see the "old you." Remember that when things get tough, you are not alone. Reach out for support and have patience with yourself and others.

P.A.T.I.E.N.C.E. ON YOUR JOURNEY

- **P**ay Attention to what's unfolding.
- **A**cknowledge your Insights.
- **T**une into your Emotions.
- **I**nterrupt Negative Thoughts.
- **E**mbrace your Challenges.
- **N**otice your Experiences.
- **E**ngage meaningfully with others.

You are stepping into a new chapter of your life—one marked by prosperity, growth, and purpose. Taking action to care for yourself or advance your career isn't selfish. You are moving toward the life you were meant to live.

CHAPTER TAKEAWAYS

- It can be harder to receive what we desire—admiration, acknowledgment, opportunities—than to give because receiving requires vulnerability.
- Giving can feel safer because it seems like we are in control, but growth comes when we lean into the discomfort of receiving.
- Change is uncomfortable, but stay with it. Replace negative self-talk with empowering beliefs.
- Honest feedback, even when painful, is a profound catalyst for growth.
- Trust yourself. You are not an imposter. Rely on your intuition and good judgment.

NUGGET FROM THE HEART

Let go of control—you never had it to begin with. Trust in your higher self.

FOR YOUR JOURNAL

1. Is it easier for you to give rather than receive? If yes, why do you think that is?
2. How has letting go of control helped you in your life?

Living Richly Bonus Practices

Sometimes, *Living Richly* means stepping into the unknown and cherishing the connections that bring joy to your life. These bonus practices will guide you toward greater abundance, clarity, and gratitude.

CHAPTER BONUS: RECEIVING AN OPPORTUNITY

Opportunities often appear when we least expect them, pushing us beyond our comfort zones. When one comes your way, take a moment to pause and assess:

- What is the risk if I proceed?
- Are there more positives than negatives in saying yes?
- Is this the right season in my life to take this leap?

If your answers lean toward "yes," it's likely a risk worth taking—more on that in chapter fifteen. The richest lives are built not by staying safe but by daring to grow. Trust that you'll gain wisdom, even if the outcome isn't what you anticipated.

RECEIVING A GIFT

Gratitude and generosity open the door to abundance.

1. Close your eyes and picture your best friend by your side.
2. Imagine you are granted two wishes:
    - First, to manifest something wonderful for your friend.
    - Second, to manifest something significant for yourself.

3. Visualize the two of you celebrating these gifts together, laughing and enjoying life.

Tuck this vision into your heart and call on it whenever you need to reconnect with joy, gratitude, or hope.

CHAPTER 5

❧

BEING FULFILLED, NOT SELFISH

When we come from our power we have an impact in the lives of others, and are fulfilled.

*L*et's get one thing straight: *achieving your goals is not selfish.* When you step into your power and pursue what you deserve, you're not just transforming your life—you're becoming a living example for others to follow. People will see your courage, success, and authenticity and be inspired to reach for more in their personal and work lives.

In the last chapter, we talked about the importance of receiving. That includes going after what you want, being acknowledged for your contributions, asking for what you need, and setting boundaries when necessary. But as I've said, many of us, especially women, were taught from a young age to be modest, to downplay our accomplishments, and to avoid confrontations.

But false modesty isn't humility; it's self-sabotage. Pretending you don't want recognition or success, especially in business, isn't noble; it's a denial of your potential. *Living Richly* means stepping out of that mindset and embracing who you are. You have the courage to do that in all areas of your life because you are fulfilled and look to contribute when you can.

SELFISH VS. FULFILLED: HERE'S THE DIFFERENCE

Take these examples.

Selfish

Your team is struggling to find a solution to a problem, you know the answer but sit back, thinking someone else will come up with it. Let them take the glory or the flak!

Fulfilled

You know the answer to the problem the team is discussing. No one asks your opinion, but you assert yourself and offer a strategy.

Selfish

Your friend's birthday is coming up, and she's planning a karaoke night. You've got the best voice in the group, and she's counting on you to kick things off. But someone offers you a free ticket to a show you've been dying to see. You bail on the birthday plans and promise to meet her later in the week instead.

Fulfilled

You're disappointed that you missed the show, but your friend's birthday is important. You show up to celebrate with her, and even though singing first is out of your comfort zone, you do it because it makes her happy.

Selfish

Your aunt is gravely ill and asks you to visit her in another state. She wants you to bring your new book and read it to her. You tell her you're too busy at work, but you just don't want to make the effort.

Fulfilled

Even though you've lost touch over the years, you know this visit will mean the world to her. You rearrange your schedule, spend time with her, and even record an extra chapter to leave behind.

THE STRUGGLE TO BE ASSERTIVE

That conflict hit me hard during a keynote speech I gave at a Midwest conference. The topic? How to be more assertive and advance in the workplace.

But as I spoke, I noticed people squirming in their seats. Later, I found out why: speaking up for yourself in that room was seen as "bragging," and bragging wasn't acceptable.

If you relate to this discomfort, here's a strategy to shift your mindset.

THE ART OF SELF-PROMOTION

There's nothing wrong with taking pride in what you've accomplished. When you're recognized for your work, acknowledge your team *and* your own contributions. For example:

"I got the buy-in from our C-Suite leaders to implement the advertising plan I created, and my team hit every benchmark enthusiastically.[*]"

See what happened there? You shared your role in pitching the project while crediting your team for their execution. It's subtle, effective, and powerful.

Living Richly means owning your wins and sharing your gifts without apology. It's not about being arrogant—it's about being authentic. *When you're fulfilled, you can give, achieve, and inspire more.*

So, step into your power. And remember, you're not just changing your life; you're showing others what's possible.

---

[*] Helene Lerner, *The Confidence Myth, Why Women Undervalue Their Skills and How to Get Over It* (California: Berrett-Koehler, 2015), 74-75.

Living Richly Practice
Let People Know Your Best

If you've achieved something you feel good about, write down the accomplishment, giving yourself credit while acknowledging others who contributed. Then, practice saying it in front of a mirror. Yes, it might feel awkward at first, but the more you do it, the more natural it will become.

I designed this exercise early in my career when I worked for a major newspaper. My male boss had a knack for making sure everyone knew about his and our team's accomplishments. Watching him, I realized I needed to do the same. I started practicing in front of a mirror,* and within a few weeks, I found it much easier to own my wins.

Now, I make it a habit to highlight something I'm proud of whenever I meet new business contacts. It's not about arrogance—it's about honoring the value of your contribution. Playing it safe and staying silent doesn't serve you or anyone else. What you've accomplished is valuable, and people need to hear it.

PLAYING IT SAFE VS. TAKING CREDIT

Here's what it looks like to stop playing small and start stepping into your power:

Playing It Safe:

"I keep quiet at meetings because a few regulars dominate the conversation."

---

* Helene Lerner, *The Confidence Myth, Why Women Undervalue Their Skills and How to Get Over It* (California: Berrett-Koehler Publishers, 2015), 75.

Taking Credit:

"If I don't speak up, no one will know about my team's contributions and how I helped make them happen."

Playing It Safe:

"I'll stick to the people I know at the cocktail party—it's easier to talk with them."

Taking Credit:

"Even though I'm nervous, I'll introduce myself to someone new, learn about their story, and share mine."

Playing It Safe:

"I do a lot of work behind the scenes for my kids' school. No one knows how much effort it takes, but I hope someone acknowledges my contribution."

Taking Credit:

"When another parent was recognized for her volunteer work, I stood up, congratulated her, and let the group know about the work I've done with others as well."

WHY IT'S IMPORTANT

When you stay silent about your efforts, you withhold a part of yourself. If you expect others to notice without saying anything, you're setting yourself up for frustration and resentment.

Take Gale, for example. She felt unappreciated by her family, rarely thanked for her efforts, and often taken for granted. But Gale didn't realize what part she was playing in this.

Her daughter, Donna, noticed her unhappiness at a Sunday dinner and called her the next day. "Mom," Donna said, "you do so much for all of us and never ask for anything. I really appreciate you."

Those words brought tears to Gale's eyes. For the first time in a long while, she allowed herself to take in the love.

At the next family dinner, Gale jokingly said, "Hey guys, how about a thank you for this amazing meal?" To her surprise, her family didn't just thank her; they stood up and hugged her.

DON'T SIT WITH IT

What's weighing on you right now? Is it feeling unappreciated, frustrated, or maybe something deeper? Ask yourself: *What am I holding back that I should be saying?* Once you've identified it, share your insights with a trusted friend and work together to plan your next move.

Acting in a new way can feel uncomfortable, but don't let that discomfort derail you. Push through and keep moving forward.

THE ONE RELATIONSHIP THAT LASTS A LIFETIME

The person guaranteed to be with you for your entire life is *you*. Isn't it time to treat yourself with the same grace and care you'd offer a dear friend?

Living Richly Practice
Spot What You Are Feeling

Throughout your day, check in with yourself, whether at work or at home. This practice is especially crucial on days when you're not at your best.

Ask yourself, "How am I doing?"

1. Accept your feelings. Don't judge your sadness, doubt, or fear. Let them exist without resistance, knowing they won't last forever.

2. Treat yourself with kindness. Imagine how you'd comfort a child— do that for yourself, too!

3. Practice patience. Allow yourself time to move through any discomfort.

4. Don't overthink it. Trying to analyze why you feel bad often leads to exhaustion. Acceptance will serve you better.

CHAPTER TAKEAWAYS

- False modesty has no place in your personal or career life.
- The time to "play it safe" is over. Step up and take credit for what you've accomplished.
- The most important relationship you'll ever have is the one with yourself. Be gracious, patient, and kind.

NUGGET FROM THE HEART

Taking care of ourselves isn't a luxury; it is necessary and something we need to do every day.

FOR YOUR JOURNAL

1. Are you frustrated because you are not getting the recognition you deserve? If yes, why do you think this is happening?
2. Think of a person you admire. How do they let people know about their accomplishments? Specifically, what do they do?
3. What is one action you could take to practice self-promotion at work?

CHAPTER 6

BEING GRACIOUS

Coming from a full heart cannot be measured in dollars and cents—it finds its value in a new currency of kindness and connection.

Graciousness is the fuel that powers the Second Key of *Living Richly*: **Getting More** of what you want. It starts with a generosity of spirit, a kindness that flows outward but begins deep within.

So, let me ask you: *Would you consider yourself a gracious person?*

How you treat others often mirrors how you feel about yourself. When you criticize others, you're likely being just as harsh with yourself. I know this firsthand because I was not gracious when I began my spiritual journey decades ago. My friend Brian woke me up with feedback that forever shifted my perspective.

THE WAKE-UP CALL

Brian noticed a pattern in me—criticism of others and myself. One day, he confronted me. He did not sugarcoat it:

"Helene, you seem unhappy. For you, the glass is half empty, not half full. You are quick to see what is wrong in people but slow to see what's right. You are missing the beauty of life and the care people show you every day.

Think about it: Did you notice the flowers in the planters this morning as you walked down the street? When friends or acquaintances help you, is your 'thank you' genuine? And when you do something good for yourself, do you give yourself credit, or do you brush it off?"

His words hit hard. At first, I felt defensive, but deep down, I knew he was right.

Brian didn't just stop pointing out the problem; he gave me a challenge. "For one week," he said, "I want you to notice the people who do *little things* for you. Write them down. At the end of the week, let's talk again."

I took him up on it, and let me tell you—it was transformative.

FROM CRITICISM TO CONNECTION

By the end of that week, I had pages filled with moments of kindness:

- The checkout lady at the supermarket smiled and wished me a wonderful day.
- The mailman cheerfully said hello as he delivered the mail.
- A stranger held the door open when my hands were full.

Suddenly, these *little things* became *big things*. I felt lighter, more connected, and deeply grateful. The world had not changed; I had.

ACTS OF KINDNESS: OPEN YOUR EYES

Brian's challenge opened my heart to the goodness all around me. Now, I am challenging you to do the same. Be on the lookout for acts of kindness happening to you every day. Graciousness is not just about grand gestures —it's about recognizing the small moments that make life beautiful.

Here are some examples to guide you. They may not match your exact experiences, but they'll give you the idea:

- **A Baby's Laughter:** Have you taken in the pure joy of a toddler giggling? That sound can soften even the hardest day if you let it in.
- **A Co-Worker's Greeting:** Did you *hear* the warmth in a co-worker's "Good morning" as you walked into the office? Or did you brush it off without a second thought?
- **Your Adult Child's Help:** When your son took out the garbage without being asked, did you stop to acknowledge him with genuine appreciation?
- **A Stranger's Gesture:** The person who picked up the paper you dropped on the street—did you thank them with a smile that conveyed your appreciation?
- **Customer Service Dedication:** When a phone company rep stayed on the line until your issue was fully resolved, did you recognize their effort and say, "Thanks for being so thorough"?
- **Your Partner's Thoughtfulness:** Did you notice the kindness in your partner's action when they picked up groceries so you could rest?

These moments are easy to miss, but when you open your eyes and heart, you see they are fueled by generosity. The *little things* in life are really *big things.*

Living Richly **Practice**
Make Graciousness Your Priority

Graciousness is a skill—it grows with practice. Start small:

1. Notice the Good: Look for at least three acts of kindness or beauty around you every day. Write them down.

2. Acknowledge Kind Acts: Don't just notice—acknowledge. Say "thank you" like you mean it, whether it is to a stranger, a friend, or a family member.

3. Celebrate Yourself: When you unexpectedly extend yourself, give yourself credit.

BE THE RIPPLE

Here is the magic of graciousness: It does not stop with you. When you show kindness and gratitude, you inspire others to do so as well. You create a ripple effect of positivity that spreads farther than you can imagine.

But acting like this also requires courage. Not everyone will appreciate your good vibes. Keep going anyway. When you live with a full heart, you are not just changing your world; you're changing the world for others who need your example.

Living Richly **Practice**
A Circle of Kindness

Just for today, notice everyone who shows you kindness. It could be someone who greets you warmly, fixes something you need, or offers help when you least expect it. Jot down what happened and how it made you feel.

At the end of the day, read your list. Then close your eyes and imagine all those people standing in a circle around you, their kindness feels like a warm embrace. Let their actions inspire you to pay it forward.

WHAT STOPS US FROM BEING GRACIOUS?

Why is it so hard to take in the "good stuff" and allow ourselves to be gracious? Too often, destructive habits close us off from the richness of life. Once we become aware of these patterns, we can take opposite actions to reclaim our joy and gratitude. Let us explore a few:

DESTRUCTIVE HABIT: JAMMING TOO MANY ACTIVITIES INTO THE DAY

When life moves too fast, we miss the beauty around us. We race from one task to another, never pausing, and wonder why we feel drained, depressed, or exhausted.

LEILA'S STORY

Leila was in her late forties, juggling two jobs to make ends meet. She lived alone, and each morning felt like life was an uphill battle. "It shouldn't be this hard to survive," she thought, dragging herself out of bed. Her friends grew increasingly worried about her; they saw the toll it took and feared she might do something drastic.

One evening, they gathered at her home and shared their concerns. Their love and honesty touched Leila deeply, prompting her to contact a therapist she had not seen in years.

In therapy, Leila confronted a truth she had been avoiding: the grief of losing her mother during COVID-19. She realized her second job had been a way to stay busy and avoid her pain. With her therapist's guidance, she let go of the second job, started freelancing for extra income, and permitted herself to grieve. Today, Leila feels more grounded and more present.

***Living Richly* Practice**
Getting Off the Treadmill

Do you overload your to-do list? I used to pack mine with so many items that it was impossible to finish them all. By the end of the day, I felt like a failure. What changed? I started prioritizing.

Step 1: Write your to-do list for today.

Step 2: If it has more than five items, move the rest to tomorrow unless one of the items is more important, and then exchange it.

Step 3: Tackle one task at a time. After finishing one, *pause* and take a deep breath before moving on to something else.

The pandemic left a mark on all of us. With having too much to do, burnout, mental health challenges, and exhaustion are widespread—and no, a quick vacation will not fix it.

The solution? Consistent self-care. Time to be gracious with yourself! Juggling work, childcare, eldercare, and everything else is not easy, and your balloon will burst if you don't take time to recharge.

Think of yourself as an accordion. You expand outward, giving your energy to work, family, and community. But to keep playing beautifully, you must also contract—pause, regroup and recharge.

DESTRUCTIVE HABIT: LETTING NEGATIVE PEOPLE GET THE UPPER HAND

The company you keep shapes your mindset and energy. Negative people can drain your spirit and pull you away from *Living Richly*.

QUESTIONS TO ASK YOURSELF

- Do the people around me support my growth, or do they hold me back?
- Are my relationships balanced, or am I doing all the giving?
- Do I receive encouragement, or am I met with constant criticism?

If you are surrounded by negativity, it's time to make a change. This might mean creating distance from "friends" who do not have your best interests at heart or even stepping back from certain family members or coworkers.

HOW TO LET GO

1. **Recognize the Impact:** Acknowledge how these relationships affect your mental and emotional health.
2. **Seek Support:** Share your feelings with trusted people who can help you navigate this shift.
3. **Create Distance:** It takes courage, but holding on to toxic connections costs far more than the discomfort of letting go.

SYLVIA'S STORY: LETTING GO OF WHAT NO LONGER SERVES YOU

Sylvia had a small circle of close friends she had known since grade school. They often spent weekends together, and for years, it felt comfortable—until it did not. The group leader, Maggie, was sharp, funny, and commanding, but her sarcasm often veered into outright criticism.

One weekend, Sylvia shared exciting news: she had an interview for a senior position at her company. It was a big stretch, and she was nervous but hopeful. Maggie, however, did not share her enthusiasm. Instead, she dismissed Sylvia's aspirations, saying she did not have the skills for the job. Maggie's reaction made it clear she wasn't happy for Sylvia.

When Sylvia landed the promotion, Maggie did not say a word—not a single "congratulations." Sylvia began to question their friendship. Maggie could be entertaining at times, but more often, she was not great company.

Feeling uneasy, Sylvia sought advice from her pastor, who suggested she take a break from Maggie. "Don't see her for a month or two," he said. "You may not even miss her. See what happens."

Sylvia followed his advice. As weeks turned into months, she realized her life felt lighter without Maggie's negativity. That friendship had been dragging her down.

DESTRUCTIVE HABIT: NOT WORKING ON AREAS THAT NEED IMPROVEMENT

To live richly, you must embrace all of yourself and know your strengths as well as areas for growth. Denying these truths about what isn't working keeps you stuck, disconnected, and unable to move on. Awareness, on the other hand, opens the door to transformation.

- Do you allow yourself time to prioritize and act on what is important to you?
- Do you admit when you have been overly critical of yourself and look toward changing that?
- Do you give yourself the proper time to replenish when you are depleted without feeling guilty?
- Do you take credit for actions you have done well?

Get honest. Where do you need to grow?

DESTRUCTIVE HABIT: BEING INAUTHENTIC

Why do we hide in the background? Why do we mask our true feelings instead of letting others see who we really are? Being authentic takes courage, and we often fear how others might react. But here is the truth: when we "people-please" to avoid conflict, others often sense our inauthenticity anyway.

CHARLENE'S STORY

Charlene was intimidated by colleagues who spoke their minds at work. She avoided conflict, even when she disagreed. During meetings, she would stay silent, convincing herself that her opinion would not make a difference.

After one meeting, her supervisor confronted her: "Charlene, I can tell you are upset about the new procedure. Why didn't you say anything?"

Charlene hesitated before admitting, "It would not have mattered. You all would have moved forward anyway."

Her boss surprised her by responding, "You have been here the longest, and you know what's needed. I would have supported you."

Though skeptical, Charlene agreed to voice her concerns in the future. Although taking that step was not easy, it marked the beginning of her journey toward authenticity.

Living Richly Practice
Speak Up

• When you feel hesitant to speak up, remind yourself that your perspective matters.

• Start small: share your honest opinion in low-stakes situations and build from there.

• Remember, your authenticity inspires others to be real too.

DESTRUCTIVE HABIT: WE ARE OUR OWN WORST CRITICS

How often do we belittle ourselves? Probably too often. Self-criticism only serves to undermine us and our goal is to be gracious.

When that inner critic shows up, here is a way to quiet its voice: replace criticism with compassion. Take these examples:

FROM CRITICISM TO COMPASSION

Criticizing:

> "I have made that mistake twice. Don't I know better?"

Showing Compassion:

> "Okay, I did it again, but next time, I will handle it differently."

Criticizing:

> "There's too much to do, and I can't relax now!"

Showing Compassion:

> "I've done a lot. Time for a break. I will just take it!"

Criticizing:

> "I feel guilty for not spending enough time with my son."

Showing Compassion:

> "I'm with my son often, and when I can't be, my mom steps in. I know, if there is ever an emergency, I will be there no matter what."

NATALIE'S STORY: MOMENTS THAT QUIET THE INNER CRITIC

Sometimes, it takes the people closest to us to remind us we are doing enough, even when our inner critic says otherwise. Natalie's story is proof of this.

Natalie was a great mother—dedicated, loving, and always striving to be there for her twin teenage daughters. She worked full-time, attended most of their important events, threw them a fantastic Sweet Sixteen party, and even served as an assistant coach for their soccer team. But she wasn't perfect—because who is?

She often felt guilty when work prevented her from being present for something special. Yet, she had raised her daughters to be strong and independent, and they thrived even when she was not by their side.

Then, on Mother's Day, Natalie received a powerful reminder of her worth. Her daughters gifted her a basket of lavender toiletries and a heartfelt card that read:

"Mom, we know you sometimes feel that you should be with us more. But you raised us to be strong, and we get that quality from you. So do not worry; we are fine. We would not change a thing about you. You are the best!"

In that moment, Natalie realized that being gracious toward herself—accepting her efforts as enough—was just as important as the love she poured into her daughters.

GRACIOUSNESS IS AT THE HEART OF A RICH LIFE

Life's richest moments are often the simplest ones shared with the people we love. Being gracious means letting those around you know they matter —your family, friends, and coworkers.

Graciousness also requires letting go of perfectionism. Constantly focusing on what isn't working in a relationship or situation is destructive and creates unnecessary misery. Instead, shift your focus to what *is* working.

SHIKIRA'S STORY: PRAISE TURNS THE TIDE

Shikira, a department store manager, struggled with an employee who seemed disengaged and unresponsive to her requests. Frustrated, she turned to her own manager for advice.

Her manager gave her a simple task: find three things the employee accomplished each day for one week and praise him for them. By the end of the week, the employee had become much more cooperative and aligned with Shikira's goals. Her willingness to be gracious unlocked the potential for connection and productivity.

CHAPTER TAKEAWAYS

- Like an accordion, we need to expand by giving of ourselves but also contract by resting, reflecting, and recharging.
- Acts of kindness, no matter how small, are truly life's greatest treasures.
- Habits like inauthenticity, self-criticism, and cramming too much into your day block the richness of life.
- Practices that deepen self-awareness foster self-intimacy and help us live more authentically.
- Showing compassion for yourself and others is the foundation of a gracious lifestyle.

NUGGET FROM THE HEART

You are worthy of praise, not criticism. Never let anyone—yourself included—put you down.

FOR YOUR JOURNAL

1. What does graciousness mean to you?
2. What barriers prevent you from getting to know yourself better?
3. What actions can you take to overcome these barriers?

CHAPTER BONUS: MINI REFRESHERS

No matter how busy life gets, quiet, reflective, and fun moments are essential. These mini refreshers allow you to recharge. Here are a few ideas to inspire you:

- Stand by a river or lake and watch the water flow. Let its rhythm calm you.

- Marvel at the intricate beauty of a butterfly—nature's living jewel.
- Twirl around your living room to your favorite song. Dance like nobody's watching!
- Hide coins around your house and invite a child on a treasure hunt.
- Laugh hysterically with a friend until tears stream down your face.

Incorporating even one of these moments into your day will serve as a "pick-me-up."

Enjoy!

THE THIRD KEY

GAINING MOMENTUM

It's time to claim your prosperity, your joy, your purpose. There is no time to waste—this is your moment to step forward and *Live Fully*.

CHAPTER 7

❦

SOUL POWER

Everything that happens to you—both good and bad—shapes
the mosaic of your life, making it uniquely yours.

When we quiet our minds, we access a deeper part of ourselves. This is where the magic happens. It's the space of intuition, connection, and clarity—our soul power. When you tap into this multidimensional realm, you're not just living your day-to-day life. You're operating from a higher plane.

LIVING IN THE REALM OF SOUL POWER

From this sacred space, you can:

- Think clearly and approach decisions calmly and with confidence.
- Speak from your heart, influencing others with authenticity and purpose.
- Lead with a spirit of service, seeing what's truly needed in the moment.
- Build consensus where others see only division.

- Empower those around you, not just with words but through your example.

This is the power of the soul—it transcends what you know intellectually and guides you to what's right.

SOUL POWER AT THE CORE OF YOUR LIFE

Imagine a circle. At the center is your soul space, radiating outward into every segment of your life: family, friends, work, and hobbies. From this core, soul power informs every decision you make, every connection you form, and every step you take.

Your soul power provides clarity in moments of uncertainty. It transcends logic, offering direction when nothing else seems clear.

EXAMPLES OF SOUL POWER IN ACTION

- A stranger asks for help, and instead of hesitating, you instinctively know how to support them.
- You're miles away from your child, but something feels off. You call the babysitter and discover they need your intervention.
- In the middle of a workplace crisis, when everyone else is scrambling, your inner guidance knows the next step.

- After fifty sales calls end in rejection, you have the strength to dig deep, knowing the next call might be the "yes" that changes everything.

ANNIE'S STORY: GUIDED BY SOUL POWER

Annie had worked the same job for 20 years and was debating whether to take early retirement. She felt torn: Should she stay in the security of her role, or was it time for a new chapter?

Her answer came unexpectedly. One day, her adult daughter mentioned plans to spend the summer in Scotland, exploring the countryside and visiting castles. Annie felt a sudden spark of excitement. She wanted to go too—but how could she take an entire month off work?

The following day, during her prayer practice, Annie heard the words: *"It's time."* That was all she needed. Guided by her soul power, she gave notice at her job. Her colleagues were sad to see her go, but Annie knew it was the right decision.

She embarked on her new adventure, traveling to Scotland with her daughter and committing to a life focused on family, exploration, and abundance.

TRUSTING IN DIVINE GUIDANCE

Soul power doesn't require you to have all the answers. It asks you to trust and have faith in the unseen, positive force working through you in your favor. This is the foundation of *Living Richly*: believing there is an inner knowing, guiding you to your highest good.

Living Richly **Practice**
Challenging Situations Can Work Out

Write down at least three times when you thought a situation wouldn't work out in your favor—and it did. Reflect on what shifted to turn things around.

Life becomes infinitely more manageable when we trust that even the most challenging situations can be resolved. Faith transformed a dark moment for Naomi and changed her hardcore beliefs.

NAOMI'S STORY

Naomi, a scientist, didn't believe in anything she couldn't observe or measure. But one evening, her faith in the unseen was awakened.

Walking home from a pub after dinner, Naomi felt someone following her. Fear kicked in. The footsteps behind her quickened as hers did. With no one else on the street to turn to, she whispered under her breath, *"Help me, God."*

At that exact moment, a patrol car turned the corner. The figure trailing her fled. Was it coincidence, or was something greater at play? Naomi's experience made her open to believing in ways she hadn't before.

FAITH VS. DISBELIEF: A TALE OF TWO MINDSETS

Faith invites us to believe in a larger view, while disbelief narrows our perspective. Consider these comparisons:

Faith:

> When we meet a new person, we trust there's a reason for the connection. We look for the opportunities they bring into our lives.

Disbelief:

> We dismiss meetings as random and assume relationships happen by chance.

Faith:

> We feel an inner nudge not to proceed with a work project, even without a logical explanation, and we trust our intuition.

Disbelief:

> We ignore our instincts, push ahead, and face the fallout when the project fails.

Faith is the bridge between uncertainty and purpose. It allows us to see problems as stepping stones, not barriers.

***Living Richly* Practice:**
Create Your Reality

Choose one concern and visualize the situation working out exactly as you'd like. Be specific. Picture who is with you, what's happening, and how you feel. For one week, upon waking, hold this image in your mind.

SMART WOMEN LIVE RICHLY

LEADING WITH SOUL POWER

As we tap into soul power, we find clarity and calm even in chaos. We may find ourselves taking on a leadership role.

Here are some real-life examples:

- **In a heated school board meeting,** tensions rise, but you wait for the right moment to offer a solution most can agree on.
- **A nephew with mental health challenges** visits you in distress. Instead of giving advice, you listen and reassure him with your calming presence.
- **Fear spreads at work** as rumors of layoffs circulate. You remind your coworkers that they're resourceful and capable. Nothing has happened yet; you'll face it together if it does.

Soul power keeps you grounded despite what is going on around you.

ALI'S STORY: HUMOR AS A TOOL

At 44, Ali underwent life-threatening heart surgery—an experience that shifted her entire perspective. Facing mortality gave her clarity: most worries weren't worth the stress.

After her surgery, she became the calming force in her office. No matter the crisis, she'd remind her group, *"This too shall pass, probably by tomorrow,"* often laughing as she said it. Her humor lightened their mood and kept everyone calm for the moment.

Living Richly Practice:
Is It Really Worth Worrying About?

When a potential crisis arises, pause before reacting. Take a deep breath and ask yourself, *"Am I making a mountain out of a molehill?"* Most of the time, you'll realize the issue isn't as significant as it seems.

SOUL POWER VS. EGO

Throughout the day, spot-check your motives: are you acting from soul power or ego? Here are some examples:

From Soul Power:

> Your son cancels plans at the last minute. You go on with your day and call him later, calmly asking for more notice next time.

From Ego:

> You're angry, feeling disrespected. Next time he asks for something, you plan to say no out of spite.

From Soul Power:

> Your grandmother invites you for dinner. Knowing you're trying to lose weight, you plan to politely decline second helpings, regardless of her response.

From Ego:

> You feel she's sabotaging your efforts to lose weight, so you skip dinner altogether, upsetting the family.

From Soul Power:

> Your boss takes credit for your report in front of leadership. After the meeting, you address what happened and ask how he plans to rectify it.

From Ego:

> You are resentful and gossip about the situation with coworkers.

Soul power invites calm, clarity, and constructive action. Ego leads to frustration and poor decisions.

SETBACKS ARE PART OF GROWTH

No matter how connected you are to soul power, setbacks will come. This isn't failure; it's human nature. When you accept this, it becomes easier to keep moving forward. Take Marguerite as an example.

MARGUERITE'S STORY: TELLING THE TRUTH AND RECEIVING HELP

Marguerite was the chief administrator of a church in the Midwest. Her role required her to support the minister and manage the congregation, tasks she handled with grace and dedication. Under her guidance, the church ran smoothly, and her usual demeanor was calm and positive.

But recently, a disgruntled congregant tested her patience. He was upset about a broken stained-glass window that hadn't been replaced. Marguerite assured him it would be fixed within the month, but that answer wasn't good enough for him. Frustrated, he called the church office six times in a single day, demanding to speak to the minister.

The repeated calls left Marguerite upset and overwhelmed. The minister, noticing her distress, asked what was wrong. After listening, he gave her this advice:

"Marguerite, you are doing your best, and we cannot please everyone. This congregant is out of line. If he calls again, tell him what I said and go on with your work. He can choose to worship at another church if this is such a problem for him."

Hearing this, Marguerite felt immediate relief. She stepped into the sanctuary, prayed, and let the situation go. Recentered and reassured, she moved on to the next task on her list.

SUPPORT AND REFLECTION

Marguerite's story highlights a simple but powerful truth: in times of stress, the guidance of someone you trust can help you refocus and regain your strength. Whether support comes from others or from within, wise counsel is always available.

Living Richly Practice:
Reflect and Get Grounded

When life feels overwhelming, stop what you're doing and find a quiet place to be alone.

1. Take a deep breath and go within. Close your eyes or simply lower your gaze.

2. Continue to breathe deeply, allowing your mind to get still.

3. Remind yourself: *The answer to my situation is coming.*

This simple practice of pausing and reflecting will help you re-energize and use your time productively.

THE SECRET INGREDIENT TO LIVING RICHLY: SOUL POWER

Soul power is the key to *Living Richly*. It is the quiet strength that comes from allowing your heart and intuition to lead. It's the faith that even when you don't have all the answers, a positive force is working within you—for you.

In the next chapter, you'll be encouraged to think bigger about what you can achieve, envision your life as you would like it to be, and never doubt what you are capable of achieving.

CHAPTER TAKEAWAYS

- Quieting your mind connects you with your core, intuition, and soul power.
- Everything in your life emanates from your soul space. Intuition can provide clarity about what's needed in any situation.
- Trusting in soul power means you don't need to have every answer in place.
- Faith is believing in the unseen. There is a positive force that will guide you when the way seems unclear.

NUGGET FROM THE HEART

Your soul is evolving. Enjoy the ride!

FOR YOUR JOURNAL

1. What enables you to trust that everything will be okay, even when you have no practical signs that it will?
2. Do you have a concept of a higher power? If so, describe what it is.
3. When was the last time you reached out for help? Describe what happened.

CHAPTER 8

THINKING BIGGER!

You are stronger than your fears, and far greater than your
accomplishments, or anyone else's opinion of you.

The era of COVID-19 turned our world upside down. Together, we've faced profound losses and shared moments of collective grief. Yet, amid the chaos, we've also demonstrated incredible resilience.

Still, the challenges of the pandemic have left many of us with shorter fuses. Things we may have once tolerated—being treated poorly, staying in unfulfilling situations—now feel unbearable. That's a good thing. It means we're waking up to the fact that *we deserve better.*

But awareness alone isn't enough. Recognizing your worth is only half the battle. The real transformation comes when you act based on that conviction.

REFLECTING ON YOUR LIFE

Ask yourself these powerful questions:

- Are you taking actions to change situations that don't foster your growth?
- Are there friendships you hold on to even though you've outgrown them?
- Have you reached a plateau in your job but stayed because you're afraid to seek something better?

These questions aren't easy to answer, but they're essential. Holding on to people, places, and things that no longer serve us drains our vitality. It's like keeping one foot in the past while trying to step into the future—you can't move forward until you let go.

TRADING YOUR POWER FOR COMFORT

We trade authenticity for comfort when we cling to outdated relationships or situations. As we discussed in Chapter Two, this often leads to adopting a false persona—a limited version of ourselves. We hide our full power because stepping into it can feel risky. But the price of staying small is far greater than the discomfort of growth.

Imagine a water faucet. If it's clogged, only a trickle of water comes out. Now consider this analogy: the water represents your abilities. If your "faucet" is clogged—by fear, self-doubt, or hesitation—your talents remain untapped. Over time, this can lead to frustration, stagnation, or even depression because your gifts aren't finding an outlet for expression.

Living Richly Practice
Steps to Unclog Your Faucet

---

1. Identify Where You're Holding Back: Choose one area of your life where you're not using your full potential, personal or career, and set a reasonable goal.

2. Take Action: Commit to one action—whether it's speaking up, starting a project, or pursuing a long-held dream.

3. Share Your Intention: Tell a trusted friend or mentor to keep you accountable.

4. Prepare for Criticism: Not everyone will support you, and that's okay. Focus on the people who resonate with what you are doing.

5. Reach Out: When setbacks occur, lean on your support network to help you regain perspective.

ALICE'S STORY: FINDING HER VOICE

Alice grew up in a family with a strict rule: *"Children should be seen, not heard."* As a result, she found authority figures intimidating and kept her thoughts to herself during work meetings, even when she had valuable ideas to share.

One day, her supervisor was out sick, and she was asked to represent him at a top-level leadership meeting. During the session, a seemingly unsolvable issue came up. No one had a solution—except Alice.

Nervously, with a shaking voice, she shared her strategy. To her surprise, the room took notice. After the meeting, the CEO praised her insight. Alice left the meeting invigorated and feeling more confident in offering her opinions.

What's the worst thing that can happen if you speak up? You might get shot down. You might feel embarrassed or begin doubting yourself. But if you think the issue is important, so what? You'll recover, and at least you'll have let people know your thoughts. The alternative—keeping quiet—leaves you with regret for not saying what's on your mind.

THE PRICE OF BEING VISIBLE

When you step into the spotlight and let your voice be heard, not everyone will agree with you. That's part of the price of being visible. The urge to "people-please" may resurface—you might feel tempted to say what you think others want to hear instead of what you believe.

But here's the challenge: *trust yourself.* Stay authentic. Even if criticism arises, regroup, and remain true to your convictions. Fran's story illustrates this perfectly.

FRAN'S STORY: THE COURAGE TO SHARE

Fran was a high school teacher who loved her students but had always dreamed of writing a book. She had spent 15 years in the classroom and wanted to share her insights with a larger audience. She lacked the confidence to start for years, but as she approached her 40th birthday, she decided, *"This is the year I do it."*

Once Fran began writing, the chapters flowed, and she completed her book within a year. She self-published, hired a publicist, and soon found herself as a guest on podcasts and local television. The feedback was overwhelmingly positive—until a suburban newspaper criticized her perspective, calling it unrealistic.

Fran couldn't stop obsessing over the negative review. It overshadowed all the praise she had received. She shared her disappointment with a writers' group she trusted. One member reminded her:

"You can't please everyone. There's a price to pay for sharing your work. Some people won't like what you have to say, but that doesn't make your book any less valuable."

Those words helped Fran regain perspective. She leaned on her community and refocused on the bigger picture: her book was making a positive impact on many people's lives.

Living Richly Practice
Regaining Perspective

Criticism is inevitable, but how you respond to it makes all the difference. When someone criticizes you, pause. Take a deep breath and get still. If something they say rings true, take note. If the criticism is unwarranted or unsolicited, don't internalize it. Instead, look that person in the eye and acknowledge that you've heard them. Most of the time, their negativity reflects how they feel about themselves—not you. Let it roll right off and move on. Their problem doesn't have to become yours!

THE COURAGE TO PERSIST

Disapproval can sting, but pushing forward despite it is where transformation happens. When you choose to play big, you're stepping into a world of possibility, growth, and excitement. Playing small, on the other hand, keeps you stuck in a cycle of inaction.

Here's what playing big versus playing small looks like:

Playing Big:

> Life becomes a thrilling adventure as you explore new terrain, try new things, and take risks.

Playing Small:

> You act out of fear, which robs you of vitality and makes life feel stagnant.

Playing Big:

> You learn the art of negotiation, advocating for your needs while remaining open to compromise.

Playing Small:

> You feel isolated, unable to effectively communicate what you want or need.

Playing Big:

> Transparency deepens your relationships, allowing you to connect with others in meaningful ways.

Playing Small:

> You take on a victim mindset, feeling deprived and disconnected from the richness of life.

Living Richly Practice:
Shift from Small to Big

Visualize someone you respect who plays big; how do you think they handle criticism? The next time you are criticized, how can you practice that in your own life?

THE REWARDS FOR PLAYING BIG

When you stop shrinking yourself to fit others' expectations, life expands. You'll feel alive, energized, and connected to your purpose. Criticism won't derail you—it will become a minor bump on the road to your success.

THE POWER OF POWER FORMATIONS

I've developed Power Formations to keep us focused and proactive, even when doubts creep in or when others disapprove. Unlike affirmations, Power Formations combine mindset shifts with actionable steps. They align you with your higher self while giving you a roadmap to move closer to your goals.

Power Formations require you to confront limiting beliefs and challenge them with questions that expand your thinking. From there, you set a clear intention and commit to an action that brings you closer to your desired outcome.

EXAMPLES OF POWER FORMATIONS

Situation One: Bridging Differences

Limiting Belief:

> "James and I are so different—we have nothing in common."

Ask Yourself:

> What is one way the two of us are alike? What activity could we share?

What Do You Really Want?

> For James and me to get closer and build a connection.

Power Formation:

> "We are both swimmers. I see James and me enjoying a morning swim together."

Action:

> I will invite James to join me for a swim on Thursday morning.

Situation Two: Overcoming Resentment

Limiting Belief:

"Cecily only thinks about her own advancement. She won't help me unless it benefits her."

Ask Yourself:

Is Cecily the only one focused on advancement? Don't I want to get ahead too?

What Do You Really Want?

I would like Cecily to introduce me to her colleague, who could be a valuable business contact.

Power Formation:

"Cecily and I both rise. We collaborate. We win together."

Action:

I will ask Cecily to send an email introduction to her colleague, and in return, I will connect her to my boss, whom she is eager to meet.

Living Richly Practice:
Your Power Formation

Use this template to create your own Power Formation for someone you find challenging:

1. What is your limiting belief about this person? *(Example: "They're too busy to care about my input.")*

2. What question can you ask yourself to shift your perception? *(Example: "What if their busyness is their way of coping with an impossible deadline, and I could offer to do a task they need?")*

3. What do you really want from this person? *(Example: "For them to consider my ideas and collaborate with me on a project.")*

4. Create your Power Formation: *(Example: "I see us working together as a team, brainstorming and creating innovative solutions.")*

5. Commit to an action: *(Example: "I will set up a meeting to offer support on their current project.")*

TAKING RISKS TO LIVE ADVENTUROUSLY

Power Formations can inspire you to take risks that lead to a richer, more adventurous life. Roberta's story shows us what happens when we stop playing small and embrace the possibilities of playing big.

ROBERTA'S STORY: SAYING YES TO ADVENTURE

Roberta had promised her preteen twins a summer vacation. The easiest option was to return to a familiar bungalow colony where the family had vacationed for years. It was predictable, affordable, and safe. But what Roberta really wanted was to swim with dolphins in Hawaii.

Her kids weren't thrilled with the idea—it was far from home, unfamiliar, and more expensive. At first, Roberta was ready to dismiss the idea herself.

Her limiting beliefs crept in: "It's too expensive", "too complicated to plan," and "what if something goes wrong?"

Then she paused and asked herself, "Why am I making a case not to go? I have the money, the time, and the desire. My children and I will have an incredible experience."

That's when she took a bold step. She shouted to her kids, "No! Let's have an adventure. We're going to Hawaii!"

With determination, Roberta researched hotels and found a tour to take them to swim with dolphins. Planning a trip like this was new territory for her, but it paid off in every way. The family had a spectacular time, creating memories they'll cherish forever.

MOVING ON TO SOMETHING BETTER

When you let go of outgrown behaviors or routines, you create space for something better to enter your life. This principle guided Anita's experience.

ANITA'S STORY: EMBRACING A NEW CHALLENGE

Anita had been working as an office manager for nearly twenty years. With just six months left until retirement, she felt like a "lame duck." She was on autopilot, doing her job with ease but feeling uninspired.

Her weekends with friends were her primary source of joy—until an unexpected opportunity arrived. A business acquaintance told her about a position that would involve creating five national offices. The pay was substantial, the benefits excellent, and the challenge invigorating.

Anita's friends assumed she'd turn it down—after all, she was so close to retirement. But Anita saw it differently. She trusted her intuition and said yes. This "smart risk" reignited her sense of purpose and brought new energy into her life.

SIMPLE PLEASURES BRING DELIGHT

When you play bigger, you trust your intuition and embrace opportunities that bring joy, growth, and adventure. Ruth's story reminds us that sometimes, thinking bigger means rediscovering the simple pleasures you've put aside.

RUTH'S STORY: FINDING JOY IN MUSIC

Ruth was a social worker who loved her job but struggled with loneliness after her mother passed away. Her mother's nightly calls had been a source of comfort, and Ruth so missed them.

One evening, walking along the main street after work, Ruth noticed a piano for sale in a shop window. She hadn't played in decades but felt drawn to it. Stepping inside the store, she sat down at the piano and played a few notes. A smile spread across her face.

The next day, she bought a piano and began taking lessons. Playing music brought a new joy into her life, filling the quiet evenings with creativity and connection to her younger self.

THE PULL OF LIMITING BELIEFS

A bigger life is waiting for you, but as you take bold steps toward *Living Richly*, fears and limiting beliefs may resurface. You may feel guilty for having abundance when others don't. You may doubt that you will be able to sustain a prosperous lifestyle. The list goes on. Don't get caught in the Mad Mind-Chatter; it is only there to distract you. Pay no attention to it, and its grip will loosen.

RESURRECT WONDER

What activity have you put on the back-burner because life felt too busy? What could you do today to bring more joy and adventure into your life?

- Is there a skill or hobby you've been curious about but haven't pursued?
- Is there a dream you've shelved because it seemed impractical?
- Write it down. Commit to taking one step in the next two weeks to move toward it.

CHAPTER TAKEAWAYS

- **Courage Is Key:** It takes courage to persist when faced with disapproval, but the rewards are immense. You get to play big and unlock your potential by pushing forward instead of staying stuck playing small.
- **Use Power Formations:** Power formations are a vital tool in the *Living Richly* toolkit. They help you align with your higher self and, more importantly, commit to actions that move you closer to your goals.
- **Move through the Pull of the Past:** When you take bold steps forward, expect resistance. Fear, guilt, and limiting thoughts may resurface, but you can loosen their grip.

NUGGET FROM THE HEART

You were brought into this life to live and dream big. Use your passion and power to create impact.

FOR YOUR JOURNAL

1. Reflect on a time when you played small. Did feelings of regret, frustration, and sadness come up as a result? What specific actions can you take to play bigger starting today?
2. Consider moments when guilt kept you from pursuing joy, success, or abundance. What strategies will you use next time guilt arises so it doesn't hold you back?

CHAPTER 9

❦

BUILDING TRUST

Trust is built on consistent actions that show care, concern,
and compassion.

𝒫icture this: You're standing at a fork in the road. A stranger points you one way, claiming it's the fastest route, but something in your gut says otherwise. What do you do? If you've learned to trust your intuition, you'll follow it—and more often than not, it'll lead you in the right direction.

Trust is the foundation of every meaningful relationship—with yourself, your loved ones, or your coworkers. When you trust your intuition, guidance often appears precisely when you need it. And when others trust you, it's because you've shown up consistently, keeping your word and demonstrating genuine care.

But here's the flip side: trust is fragile. Break a promise, act inconsistently, or prioritize yourself at the expense of others, and trust dissolves. People remember how you make them feel. Without trust, relationships stall. You do the bare minimum for someone you don't trust, and they'll do the same for you.

THE BEHAVIORS THAT BLOCK TRUST

What destroys trust? These are the habits that erode connection and credibility:

- **Saying one thing and doing another.** When your words and actions don't align, trust takes a hit.
- **Being selfish.** Putting yourself first without considering others so that they can't rely on you.
- **Lack of consistency over time.** Trust isn't built in a day—it's earned through steady, dependable behavior.
- **Being pressured into doing something you don't believe in.** Being coerced to say yes undermines the belief that the person cares about you.
- **Breaking promises.** Failing to deliver on commitments chips away at the foundation of trust.

THE BEHAVIORS THAT BUILD TRUST

Now, let's look at the flip side. Trust grows when your actions consistently demonstrate reliability and care. These are the behaviors that strengthen bonds and inspire confidence:

- **Following through on commitments.** When you say you'll do something, you do it.
- **Showing genuine care for others.** You make it clear that their needs matter to you.
- **Respecting boundaries.** Healthy relationships thrive when everyone's limits are honored.
- **Being consistent.** You show up reliably, day after day.
- **Letting your word be your bond.** When people know they can count on you, trust deepens.

TRUST IN TURBULENT TIMES

Let's face it: The pandemic, new government regimes, wars, climate change, AI innovations, corporate reorganizations, and hybrid workspaces have left many of us feeling off balance. Fear of job loss, financial uncertainty, and environmental concerns, among other things, have left many of us feeling unsafe.

In these moments, trust is more crucial than ever—not just trust in others but trust in yourself. Do you believe in your ability to make decisions in your best interest? Can you rely on your intuition to guide you through the incessant "noise" during these challenging times?

This is where the *Living Richly Toolkit* comes in. Let's explore a few tools for rebuilding and strengthening trust, even when you are feeling most vulnerable.

TOOLS TO BUILD TRUST

1. **Trusting Your Intuition:** Your inner voice is a powerful guide. Pause, listen, and let it steer your decisions. Intuition often knows what logic cannot.
2. **Communicating Honestly and Openly:** Trust thrives on transparency. When misunderstandings arise, address them with honesty and compassion.
3. **Simplifying Your Commitments:** Overpromising and under-delivering is a trust killer. Instead, commit to less and ensure you follow through.
4. **Taking Consistent Action:** Small, consistent acts of care build trust over time. Show others and yourself that you can be counted on.
5. **Extending Trust to Receive It:** Trust is a two-way street. Offer trust to others, and you'll create the conditions for it to be returned.

INTUITION: A POWER TOOL

Intuition is your internal compass, a deep, quiet voice guiding you to the truth. Some call it instinct; others see it as a connection to something greater. Whatever you call it, your intuition never lies.

How many times have you ignored what your gut was telling you, only to regret it later? I know I have. Over the years, I've learned to act on my intuition, even when it doesn't make logical sense at the time. When that little voice warns me that something isn't right, I listen.

Intuition can be relied on when the right choice isn't obvious. Eileen's story demonstrates this perfectly.

DEEP DOWN, SHE KNEW IT WASN'T RIGHT

Eileen was interviewed for a managerial position at a tech company. She'd aced three interviews and was thrilled about the creative challenges the role offered. During her final interview with the CEO, everything seemed fine on the surface. But something about him didn't sit right with her. She couldn't explain why, but she felt uneasy.

Later, she called a former tech company employee who had heard that the CEO might be charged with fraud. Although the news had not yet leaked to the media, Eileen's intuition had already signaled something was wrong. She turned the offer down and avoided a potentially disastrous situation.

DON'T GET TRICKED BY THE MIND

Here's the thing: Your mind can be noisy, unpredictable, and full of stories. One moment, it's urging you forward; the next, it's holding you back with fear and doubt. That's why trusting your intuition is so important; it grounds you in reality and helps you make decisions aligned with your truth.

For example, your mind might scream, *"You'll never finish this project on time!"* But your intuition counters with calm reassurance: *"Take the next right action—you'll get there."*

When doubt creeps in, you can shift gears by reconnecting with the present moment. This practice will help you do just that.

Living Richly Practice
Trust the Guidance of the Present Moment

Your senses are your anchors to reality. Here's how to connect with them:

1. Sound: Close your eyes and focus on what you hear, near and far.

2. Sight: Open your eyes and take in the colors, shapes, and textures around you.

3. Taste: Eat or drink something. Is it sweet, sour, or salty?

4. Smell: Notice the scents in the air—subtle or strong.

5. Touch: Feel your forehead or another part of your body. Is it warm or cool?

Once you're grounded in the present moment, reflect on a situation you're grappling with. What does your intuition tell you is the right action to take? Heed its guidance.

TRUSTING YOURSELF LEADS TO LIVING RICHLY

When you trust yourself, you unlock the ability to live fully. Here's how trust leads to a richer life:

Trusting: I trust myself to show up for the people I care about.

Living Richly: Closer, more meaningful relationships with family and friends.

Trusting: I trust myself to speak up when I can make a difference.

Living Richly: Greater impact in your life and the lives of others.

Trusting: I trust myself to walk away from situations I've outgrown.

Living Richly: More energy for opportunities that align with your purpose.

Gabriele's journey is a testament to the power of self-trust.

SMALL STEPS TOWARD BIG CHANGE

"There were too many times when I went against what I knew was right," Gabriele admits. "I'd feel so angry at myself afterward. I had to change."

She started small. She said no to a fourth date because her gut told her the person wasn't right for her. She declined an extra shift at work because she was exhausted and knew she wouldn't perform well. These choices were hard at first, but they built her confidence.

"Now, I trust myself more. It's not always easy—some people don't like the changes I've made. But I realized, if someone can't accept the real me, they're not my kind of people."

TRUSTING AND MAKING AMENDS

Trusting yourself doesn't mean you won't make mistakes. You will. But *Living Richly* also means taking responsibility for those mistakes.

When conflicts arise, be willing to look at your part, not just at what the other person has done. Awareness of your triggers, combined with a genuine apology, can repair relationships and deepen trust. The following practice offers clarity on what may need to be amended.

Living Richly Practice
Get Clear with a Trust Inventory

Take out a sheet of paper and create three columns. First, write down the names of people you do not trust. In the second, reflect on why you don't trust them—what actions or patterns have created this barrier? In the third, examine your own role. What might you be doing to limit the relationship?

Now, decide if the relationships are worth saving. If any one of them is, share your observations with a trusted friend and create a course of action to restore it.

Here's an example of how two friends reconciled: Susie felt hurt by her friend Dale, who repeatedly canceled plans at the last minute. When Susie confronted Dale, she was clear: *"Friends don't treat each other this way. Canceling without a good reason, especially several times, is inconsiderate."* After reflection, Dale valued their friendship and recognized her pattern as a way of avoiding closeness. She apologized, but Susie needed time to process her feelings. Eventually, they rebuilt trust, showing that clarity and accountability can pave the way for reconciliation.

FORGIVENESS: A POWERFUL TOOL

Forgiveness is not about condoning someone's actions. It is more about releasing yourself from the burden of resentment. Letting go of the need to be "right" can feel liberating, like letting go of a block that has been weighing you down. Relationships flourish when forgiveness replaces blame.

Barbara, for example, grew up with a controlling father. Her past often caused conflict in her marriage. Recently, her husband accused her of being selfish because she neglected something important that he asked her to do. Instead of snapping back, she took a deep breath and calmly replied, *"I hear you."* Her restraint diffused the tension, and he soon apologized.

Barbara realized that choosing not to engage in unnecessary conflict preserved the peace and strengthened their bond.

Living Richly Practice
Forgiveness Mantra

Identify one person with whom you struggle to trust—if they're not already on your trust inventory, add them now. Each morning, close your eyes and visualize them achieving their goals and living joyfully. Also, repeat this several times to yourself: *I forgive you. I accept you. I wish you the best.* Resistance may arise, but remember, forgiveness isn't just for them; it's for you. It frees you to *Live Richly* and with greater emotional clarity.

It's essential to extend forgiveness to yourself. Forgive yourself for moments when you believed someone else's hurtful words or acted in ways you now regret. Self-compassion is a profound gift, a way to heal and grow from within.

Practicing empathy for yourself and others is foundational to *Living Richly*. Acknowledging your own triggers and forgiving creates space for healing and connection. Relationships deepen, trust strengthens, and emotional well-being grows, which we'll explore in the next chapter.

CHAPTER TAKEAWAYS

- Saying one thing while doing another, being selfish, and being inconsistent are examples of trust blockers.
- Behaviors that build trust are following through on commitments, showing genuine care, and respecting boundaries.
- Intuition is a powerful tool that should be followed. It is your internal compass, a deep, quiet voice guiding you to the truth.
- Forgiveness is not about condoning someone's actions. It is more about releasing yourself from the burden of resentment.

NUGGET FROM THE HEART

It takes courage to break old patterns and meet others with empathy when they hurt you. Understanding the vulnerabilities of those you care about can transform relationships.

FOR YOUR JOURNAL

1. Describe a situation when you forgave someone close to you because you knew the person who would benefit the most was you.
2. Have you been able to work through trust issues with a friend? If so, what enabled you to do this?
3. What are the ways you do not trust yourself? How can you change that?

THE FOURTH KEY

GIVING BACK

When our hearts are open, we connect with others. Giving and receiving become natural, and the greater good is served.

CHAPTER 10

❦

LIVING WITH EMPATHY AND COMPASSION

*We move from darkness to light when we remember that
despite our differences, we share the same fundamental
experiences: we are born, we live, and one day, we will die.
These truths unite us in our humanity.*

*C*ompassion is the foundation for *Living Richly*. It creates a life where joy, abundance, empathy, and love flow freely. Compassion connects us to our higher self. When we live with compassion, we lift ourselves and others up. Conversely, living from a place of fear pulls us down.

COMPASSION VS. FEAR: A COMPARISON

- **With Compassion:** Kindness becomes your natural state, and you look for the good in people.
- **With Fear:** You often look over your shoulder, fearing losing what you value.
- **With Compassion:** You have faith that something better is around the corner.

- **With Fear:** You believe nothing will change, that life is static and unyielding.
- **With Compassion:** You feel inspired to give to others who are less fortunate.
- **With Fear:** You hoard what you can, fearing there won't be enough to go around.

THE CONNECTION BETWEEN EMPATHY AND COMPASSION

Empathy allows us to feel what another person is experiencing. When combined with compassion, it propels us to act, help, and heal. Science supports this: When we're in a compassionate state, our brains release oxytocin—the "love hormone"—which strengthens our bonds with others.[*]

But what about those times when compassion feels out of reach? How do we find it when we're weighed down by stress, anger, or frustration?

AN ATTITUDE OF GRATITUDE

When you have a grateful heart, you treat others—and yourself—with more kindness and empathy. Gratitude is the gateway to compassion. It's a mindset that transforms how we approach our day, disappointments, and successes. With gratitude, we begin to hope and trust that the best is yet to come. But the question is: Do we actively practice it?

When I find myself in a funk, gratitude is my quickest way out. I start by acknowledging the negative thought or feeling that's bringing me down. Then, I shift my focus. I ground myself in the present moment by tuning into my senses and actively looking for things to be grateful for.

---

[*] "The Science of Kindness," *Cedars-Sinai Blog* (February 13, 2019), https://www.cedars-sinai.org/blog/science-of-kindness.html.

Here's a fun way to practice gratitude that can lift your spirit and open your heart. It's a simple yet transformative practice that can elevate your mood.

Living Richly Practice
Infuse Your Day with a Gratitude Chant

---

1. Find Your Rhythm: Take a drum if you have one, or simply use your hand to tap a beat on a solid surface. Create a rhythm that feels good—something you might dance to.

2. Start Chanting: To the rhythm, repeat the phrase:

"I am grateful, I am grateful, I am grateful for_____"

Then, fill in the blank with something you're thankful for. Chant at least 10 things. Go at your own pace.

Here's my Gratitude Chant:

I am grateful for:

"I enjoy good health, my son Heath, my beautiful home, my friends, the flower market in New York City, my sister Beth, my little nephew Rowan, sound sleep, Italian food, and my plants."

Feel free to move as you chant, letting the rhythm guide your body. Once you've finished, notice how you feel. You'll likely feel lighter, more energized, and ready to tackle something new.

PLEASURE IS YOUR BIRTHRIGHT

Are you taking the time to enjoy your life? When you are, your tank is full. Compassion, empathy, and generosity flow naturally from this state.

But too many of us may be chasing the next project, relationship, or conquest, leaving little room for pleasure.

Reflection is necessary if you find yourself stuck in "what's next" mode. Do you feel unworthy, not good enough? Whatever story you are telling yourself is likely untrue. It may stem from childhood, perhaps something you learned from a parent, teacher, or someone else who planted seeds of self-doubt. But that story doesn't serve you anymore. It's time to bless the past and move on.

Pleasure is your birthright. You deserve to enjoy all areas of life:

- Work you love and are paid well for.
- Relationships that nurture and support your growth.
- Time to play, laugh, and simply be.
- Opportunities to create impact in ways that feel meaningful to you.

RECEIVING PLEASURE IS NOT SELFISH

In chapter four, we saw how giving may be easier for some of us than receiving. However, allowing joy, fun, and fulfillment in our lives is so important. It helps us recharge and creates an open space for greater connection and contribution.

Now is the time to:

- **Have more fun.** Make room for laughter, play, and spontaneity.
- **Level up your career.** Seek work that excites and challenges you, and don't settle for less than you're worth.
- **Cultivate supportive relationships.** Surround yourself with people who uplift and inspire you.

As you embrace pleasure and abundance, you support others in doing the same. *Living Richly* has a ripple effect; it starts with you and spreads outward.

Living Richly Practice:
Try These on for Size

Incorporate these simple yet powerful habits into your daily life to elevate your mood, build resilience, receive pleasure and foster compassion:

• **Set intentions:** Start your day with purpose. Get up ten minutes earlier, splash cold water on your face, and take a moment to set your intention for the day.

• **Find stillness:** Once a day, find a quiet place and be still for ten minutes. Let yourself enjoy the silence and recharge.

• **Pause before reacting:** Stop and pause when someone pushes your buttons. Take a deep breath and choose not to react impulsively.

• **Replace worry:** Worrying achieves nothing. Instead, do something that brings you pleasure, a good laugh with a friend, or a favorite meal.

• **Energize a slump:** Feeling low? Get your body moving. Go for a walk or run, hit the gym, or do an at-home workout to boost your energy.

• **Revisit past successes:** When self-doubt creeps in, reimagine a moment when you accomplished something special. Relive that feeling of triumph.

• **Relieve stress:** Massage your neck or upper back. Press firmly into a tension spot for ten seconds, then release. Feel the relief as your muscles relax.

• **Deflect negativity:** If someone looks at you with disdain or anger, remind yourself that their behavior is about their inner struggles; it's not about you.

• **Give yourself a pep talk:** Reflect on what you did well at the end of each day. What can you improve on tomorrow? Endorse yourself for the effort you've put in!

THE POWER OF GRACE AND COMPASSION

I've been fortunate to have remarkable friends who embody resilience, compassion, and empathy. They've faced life's challenges with grace, showing that even in difficult times, it's possible to rise above negativity, tap into their inner strength, make meaningful connections, and practice gratitude.

Let their stories inspire you to cultivate more empathy and kindness in your life. When we approach the world with an open heart, we initiate positive changes.

STORIES OF GRACE, GRATITUDE, AND VISION

Diane: Seeing the World Through a Lens of Gratitude

Big green eyes, blonde hair, and a radiant smile—this is Diane. As a reverend, she approaches life seeing challenges as opportunities for growth. About two years ago, Diane had a serious fall while walking her dog in the botanical gardens near her home. She was rushed to the hospital, where a team of doctors and nurses cared for her.

When I called to check on her, Diane didn't dwell on the pain or the inconvenience. Instead, she focused on the kindness of the healthcare team. True to her nature, she took the time to get to know them and even offered spiritual guidance to those who needed it.

Her openness lifted the spirits of those around her and accelerated her healing. Diane's story reminds us that gratitude transforms even the most difficult experiences into opportunities for connection.

Sandy: Trusting the Highest Power

Sandy is a self-made millionaire and a shining example of compassionate leadership. Her business acumen is matched only by her desire to give back to her community. Deeply spiritual, she refers to her connection to the Divine as the "Highest Power" and credits the guidance received for getting her through times of uncertainty.

When faced with important decisions, Sandy consults with trusted friends and taps into her intuition. She considered entering a promising business deal about a year ago but felt an internal nudge to wait. Trusting that, she delayed and later discovered significant issues within the team managing the project.

Sandy appreciates life's lessons, both good and bad. She generously shares her wisdom, helping others navigate their own paths, knowing they are not alone.

Lynn: Creating a Vision and Making It Real

Lynn is a single mother of two college-age sons. She is a thriving architect who is passionate about her craft. Lynn has wanted to design and build her own home on a serene lakeside property for the longest time.

Two years ago, she purchased the land and began envisioning her future home. She spent weekends at the site, imagining every detail. Based on this vision, she drew up the plans and set to work.

Today, her dream house is a reality. The process wasn't without its challenges, but Lynn's determination carried her through. Just as importantly, she cultivates a supportive, empathetic team at her firm. Her leadership is rooted in care for her projects and her employees' career growth. Lynn's story proves that dreams are achievable with vision, empathy, and perseverance.

BRING CLARITY TO YOUR VISION

Your vision bridges where you are and where you want to be. Reflect on what you truly desire and start crafting your own *Living Richly Vision Statement*. Build it with gratitude, compassion, and an unwavering belief in yourself.

The statement can encompass health, personal relationships, work goals, or any other area of life. It is an overall declaration of where you are headed. Think of it as your "elevator pitch" to your higher self. In the next chapter, we will focus on a vision specifically for your career.

MY VISION STATEMENT

Here's an example of my own vision statement:

"I am in vibrant health. My relationships are loving and empowering. My work is impactful and inspirational to others. My life is rooted in compassion, empathy, and joyful living."

Your vision will evolve as you grow. Having it as a guiding star will keep you focused and inspired.

Living Richly Practice
Creating a Vision for Your Life

---

1. Get Comfortable: Sit in a chair where you can fully relax. Close or lower your eyes and take a few deep breaths to release any tension.

2. Reflect: *What would I like my life to look like regarding my relationships, my health, and my work?*

3. Visualize: Imagine that this is a reality. Picture yourself enjoying the different aspects of your life. How do you feel?

4. Write It Down: Open your eyes and, from a place of contentment and empowerment, write down your experience in an affirmative statement.

5. Refine and Affirm: Share your vision with someone you trust to refine it further. Then, say it aloud each morning for a month, letting it guide your actions and focus.

COURTESY: AN EXCHANGE OF GOODWILL

Courtesy isn't just about having good manners; it's about genuinely opening your heart to others. True courtesy sparks connection and ignites goodwill, empathy, and compassion.

Take this example: You see an elderly man struggling to cross the street and extend your hand to help. At that moment, you place yourself in his position. Your connection is more than a polite gesture; it's an act of shared humanity.

These small moments of goodwill can touch everyone involved, lifting not just the recipient but also your own spirit.

Living Richly Practice
Wake Up!

How often do we move through life distracted, lost in the chatter of our own thoughts? We walk down the street but miss the beauty, vibrancy, and humanity surrounding us.

The next time you catch yourself stuck in your mind chatter, try this:

1. Stop: Pause and take a deep breath.

2. Shift Gears: Turn your attention outward. What do you see? Who is around you? What sounds and smells fill the air?

3. Be Present: Notice the details—the rustling of leaves, the laughter of children, the warmth of sunlight on your skin.

By practicing presence, you connect more deeply with your environment—and the people in it.

CHAPTER TAKEAWAYS

- **Empathy and Compassion:** Empathy allows us to feel what others are going through; compassion turns that feeling into an impulse to help.
- **Gratitude:** Approaching life with gratitude creates hope and anticipation for the best outcomes, even when facing challenges.
- **Pleasure Is Your Birthright:** Enjoying life fills your tank and fuels compassion and empathy.
- **The Power of Vision:** Creating a life vision helps you focus on what truly matters, guiding you toward a richer way of living.
- **Courtesy as Connection:** True courtesy involves more than politeness. It's about a genuine exchange of goodwill.

NUGGET FROM THE HEART

A rich life is one in which empathy, compassion, and grace take over; we share our joys and challenges with other travelers we meet along the way.

FOR YOUR JOURNAL

1. Describe someone you know who embodies empathy and compassion.
2. How do you practice gratitude? If you don't, how will you, and when will you start?
3. When have you recently extended yourself to someone else? How did the person react and how did you feel?

CHAPTER 11

⚜

THE POWER OF MONEY AND ITS LIMITS

Money is a powerful tool, but it has its limits. It can buy
comfort, security, and opportunities, but it cannot buy
happiness, peace of mind, or self-respect.

THE ROLE OF MONEY IN LIVING RICHLY

*M*oney is necessary to live a prosperous life. Smart financial habits—like saving, investing wisely, living within your means, and sharing your wealth through tithing or philanthropy—help create a stable foundation. These practices allow us to maintain a rich lifestyle rooted in freedom, not fear.

The problem arises when we elevate money beyond its function. Money is simply an exchange for goods and services, not the solution to life's deeper problems. When we believe wealth will give us intangibles like happiness or fulfillment, we put money on a pedestal it doesn't deserve.

Yes, having more money can ease certain challenges. But there are countless stories of billionaires who are unhappy, lonely, or directionless. Their bank accounts are overflowing, but their souls are starving. Why? Money can't buy the things that truly matter.

Here's what money *can't* do:

- It can't buy real friends who care about you for who you are, not what you have.
- It can't create lasting confidence or self-esteem—those come from within.
- It can't replace loyalty or integrity.

Some of the richest people are those with very little in terms of material wealth, but they are abundant in kindness, generosity, and wisdom.

THE TRUE COST OF WHAT MONEY CAN'T BUY

- It costs **$0** to be kind to someone in need.
- It costs **$0** to lend a helping hand.
- It costs **$0** to de-escalate a tense situation calmly and clearly.
- It costs **$0** to bring positivity into a room.
- It costs **$0** to speak your truth when it matters most.
- It costs **$0** to walk away from a toxic or disrespectful environment.

These are the priceless currencies of life—things that no dollar amount can measure.

FEAR OF FINANCIAL INSECURITY

When we let the fear of financial insecurity rule our lives, we block ourselves from *Living Richly*. This fear can manifest in these ways:

1. **Scarcity Mindset:** Constantly worrying about not having enough, even when your needs are met.
2. **Hoarding Wealth:** Clinging to money out of fear of losing it can isolate you and limit your joy.

Both approaches can prevent you from appreciating the abundance already present in your life. Fear creates a wall between you and the flow of money and opportunity.

Ask yourself:

- Have I let the fear of not having enough money dictate my decisions?
- How has this fear kept me from appreciating what I already have?
- Can I see how my attitude toward money affects how much abundance I allow into my life?

CREATING A PROSPERITY MINDSET

Wealth creation begins with a mindset of abundance, not scarcity. The media often emphasizes external circumstances—economic downturns, market crashes, or job insecurity—but one's internal perspective has a lot to do with one's financial reality.

Take the financial crisis of 2007-2009. Many people were paralyzed by fear, but I refused to let it crush my spirit. Instead, I focused on what I *could* control: pitching sponsorships to corporate clients, doubling down on my practices to maintain a positive mindset, and staying proactive.

The result? I earned more money than in previous years and produced a successful television show. The key wasn't luck or timing; it was my decision to focus on abundance, surround myself with supportive people, and take consistent action.

Living Richly Practice
Form An Abundance Sharing Circle

• Gather a group of like-minded individuals who share a positive, prosperous outlook on life.

• Meet weekly to remind each other of the truth: external circumstances may shift, but you have the power to consistently take actions to create all that you need. This supportive network will help you stay accountable and avoid slipping back into old habits.

• Share your wins, brainstorm solutions to challenges, and support one another in maintaining a *Living Richly* mindset.

MONEY AND SELF-ESTEEM

Too often, we let the numbers in our bank accounts dictate how we feel about ourselves. When this happens, it's crucial to remember:

I am enough and have enough, right here and right now!

This mantra is a powerful tool to ground yourself in the truth. Incorporating it into your daily routine allows you to break the cycle of letting financial metrics define your self-worth.

Living Richly Practice
Taking Stock

Take a moment to reflect on everything you have—money, material possessions, close relationships, career, and personal growth.

1. Write it down: List big and small things alike.

2. Share Your List with a trusted friend to reinforce your sense of prosperity.

3. Reassure Yourself: Shift your mindset from scarcity to abundance by realizing that you have enough for today and can create more as needed.

MONEY AND THE BIGGER PICTURE

When we focus solely on material wealth, we may lose sight of what truly matters. Out of frustration, we can fall into the trap of blaming others for what we feel is lacking.

Take Shirley, for example. She criticized her partner for not earning enough to meet their family's needs, but she wasn't addressing her own unfulfilled career ambitions. Shirley had left her finance degree unfinished when she gave birth to twins, and she went from full-time to part-time at work. When we started our coaching sessions, it became clear that her dissatisfaction stemmed from her fear of returning to school and her doubts about keeping up with younger students.

With encouragement from her family and myself, Shirley took the leap, re-enrolled, and is now close to finishing her degree. She is rediscovering her sense of purpose and reigniting her ability to make a greater impact at work. The additional money she will bring in is only part of the story.

THE POWER OF IMPACT

Most of us spend a good portion of our waking hours on-the-job. If we don't contribute meaningfully, we can experience frustration, anger, and even depression. In speaking with the women I counsel, I have found that they have an overwhelming desire to make an impact at work. This is a vital component of their fulfillment.

Your work should be more than a paycheck; it should be a place where you can use your talents and skills to make a difference. We practiced setting an overall vision for your life in the previous chapter; now, we will do the same with a focus on your career. Here's a practice to help you clarify your career vision.

Living Richly Practice
Create a Career Vision

---

1. Get Comfortable: Sit in a quiet place and close your eyes or lower your gaze.

2. Reflect: Think about your current job. *Is this work making a meaningful difference in people's lives?*

3. Imagine: If the answer is no, visualize a job where you would make an impact. Are you at a different company, in the same industry, or another one? Are you doing a different job? Are you part of a team or leading a team? Who are the people you are working with?

4. Commit: Reflect on these questions for ten minutes each morning for at least two weeks to start clarifying your vision.

5. Discuss: Share your insights with a trusted friend, mentor, or career counselor to begin to flesh out your vision and strategize your next steps.

As you create or tweak your career vision, keep in mind that whatever your job, bringing your authentic self to work contributes to your success.

In our Smart Women Live Richly Survey, over 80% of respondents answered that the key to creating a rich lifestyle was being authentic and showing other people the "real you." It wasn't just about the money, and that applies to your work life as well.

Visibility is essential in your career. People need to know who you are and how your skills, services, or products can help them. However, visibility comes with vulnerability, and you might face rejection. It takes a lot of "nos" to get to that "Yes!"

But think of it this way: it's a numbers game. The more people you engage with, the closer you are to getting the desired result.

YOU DESERVE THE BEST!

Imagine this: a job where you use many of your skills and are compensated well, relationships that empower and uplift you, and a financial plan that allows you to both save and enjoy your money. All of this is within reach if you take deliberate steps toward achieving your goals.

CREATING A SAVINGS PLAN

From a young age, I was taught the importance of saving. My mother, a bank teller, set up a savings account for me, and with my babysitting money or allowance, I made small but consistent deposits. This simple habit laid the foundation for financial stability.

Contrast this with a "crash and burn" attitude—living only for today because tomorrow is uncertain. While it's true that life is unpredictable, you can have financial consistency, and saving is an essential practice, not a restriction.

If you don't already have a savings plan, now is the time to create one. Consult with a financial advisor to establish a strategy that works for you and your lifestyle.

CHAPTER TAKEAWAYS

- Money is important, but it isn't everything.
- Some of the richest people do not have the largest bank accounts because their wealth cannot be valued by material things.
- Money can't buy real friends. It can't create lasting confidence or self-esteem—those come from within. It can't replace loyalty or integrity.
- Fear of financial insecurity manifests in a scarcity mindset or hoarding wealth.
- Spend time creating your career vision. You deserve to have a job where you are respected, well-paid, and create impact.
- Being visible is important for a successful career, but it also comes with vulnerability. Not everyone will approve of you or your product. But the more "nos" you get, the closer you get to a "yes."

NUGGET FROM THE HEART

Getting clear on what you want in your career life, brings you closer to attaining it and living abundantly.

FOR YOUR JOURNAL

1. What does money represent to you?
2. Describe a time when you were so focused on making more money that you lost sight of the valuable things you already had in your life.
3. Do you have a savings plan? If not, speak to a financial advisor and start one. (Don't worry if the deposits are small at first.)

CHAPTER 12

CREATING RICH RELATIONSHIPS THROUGH COMMUNICATION AND CONNECTION

Observing how others communicate and speaking "their language" creates connection and trust.

*A*s I've said in the last chapter, money and material wealth are only part of a rich life. True abundance comes from the relationships we build and the trust we cultivate. One of the most powerful ways to foster trust is through communication. I have learned that by understanding and adapting to others' styles, especially in business, we can connect more deeply and create meaningful, long-lasting partnerships, which, not surprisingly, lead to generating income.

STEPS FOR EFFECTIVE COMMUNICATION ON THE JOB

People are more likely to engage with someone who makes them feel understood. By aligning your style with theirs, you increase receptivity.

Here are the steps to master this approach:

1. **Observe:** Pay attention to how they communicate. Do they repeat certain words or phrases?
2. **Listen Beyond Words:** Notice their mood and what they're not saying. When you quiet your own "Mad Mind-Chatter," you'll pick up on subtle cues.
3. **Express:** Use the words and phrases you've observed in your remarks. This builds rapport and shows alignment.
4. **Respond:** When they ask questions, answer in their style— whether concise or detailed.

I've used this strategy to create mutually beneficial relationships. For instance, if you're naturally a storyteller but the person you're talking to is analytical, adjust your communication style. Keep your sentences short, focus on facts, and make your "ask" quick and direct.

ISABELLA'S SUCCESS STORY: PREPARATION LEADS TO SUCCESS

Isabella was preparing to meet a high-profile prospect. She watched videos of him to study his communication style and tailored her pitch accordingly. After the meeting, she called me, thrilled with the results—a sale seemed promising, and a follow-up call was already scheduled.

COMMUNICATION STYLES: THE KEY TO CONNECTION

Adapting to someone's style isn't about compromising yourself; it's about ensuring your message is heard. By communicating in *their* language, you'll negotiate more effectively and build stronger relationships.

There are many communication tools out there, and you may want to investigate a few. I have used a simple framework with two basic styles. They help me identify and adapt to other people, creating better connections:

1. **The Storyteller:**
   o Uses emotion to express themselves.
   o Share many details and examples.
   o Engaging, but takes time to get to the point.
2. **The "To-the-Point" Talker:**
   o Uses short, direct sentences.
   o Quickly expresses what's on their mind.
   o Not big on emotion or unnecessary details.

Living Richly **Practice**
Use Their Words

Before meeting someone new, research their communication style.

• Watch videos or podcasts featuring them. If possible, observe how they interact in real life.

• Write down repeated words, phrases, and insights about their demeanor.

• During your meeting, subtly use their words and phrases to show alignment and build rapport.

This approach demonstrates attentiveness and respect, making the other person more open to hearing your ideas.

MAKING BUSINESS FRIENDS

Trust is the foundation of any strong relationship, personal or professional. You build a relationship with a business friend based on mutual respect and care. Unlike personal friendships, business friendships might not reveal every side of you, but the core element of trust remains the same. People want to work with others who care about them—not just their results.

OBSERVE, FIND COMMON GROUND, EASE INTO BUSINESS

When I meet potential partners, I rarely dive straight into business. Instead, I ask how they're doing, offer support, and build a personal connection. Sometimes, this means scheduling a follow-up meeting to discuss business. The result? Long-term relationships rooted in trust and collaboration.

GLADYS'S STORY:

Gladys built a strong connection with a new client, Samuel, simply by showing genuine care. On their first meeting, she noticed he was recovering from a cold and gently reminded him to take it easy. This small act of kindness set the tone for a lasting professional relationship. Samuel trusted Gladys not just as a reliable vendor but as someone who was concerned about his well-being.

Relationships that start with sincerity build a foundation for long-term collaboration. One of my most rewarding business friendships started with a cold call. Over time, this relationship grew into a trusted partnership. We shared meals, cultural experiences, and conversations about family and professional goals. This trust led to sponsorships for public television shows and introductions to other key leaders. Business friends can become your greatest allies. They'll support your goals because they know you will go the extra mile to help them achieve theirs.

CHAPTER TAKEAWAYS

- Richness can't always be measured in dollars. Kindness, trust, and mutual respect in relationships are priceless.
- Communication is a powerful tool—adapt your style to the person you're speaking with to ensure your message is received.
- Building business friendships create long-term allies rooted in trust and a shared vision.
- Take time to connect personally with new prospects before diving into business. This sets the stage for a more well-rounded relationship.

NUGGET FROM THE HEART

As you build trust and foster meaningful connections, abundance flows naturally into your life.

FOR YOUR JOURNAL

1. Reflect on the communication styles of people in your family. How are they similar to or different from yours?
2. Think about your boss or an important professional contact. What is their communication style? How can you adjust your approach to align better with theirs?

THE FIFTH KEY

GOING THE EXTRA MILE

Small, consistent actions form the foundation of a rich and meaningful life. By layering powerful practices into your daily routine, you
can transform how you start your day and carry that energy forward
in everything you do.

CHAPTER 13

THE THREE C'S—CLARITY, COMMITMENT, &
CONTINUOUS ACTION

Life will throw us curves, but in our darkest moments, we find
a wellspring of strength we never knew we had.

$\mathcal{C}$hallenging times reveal our resilience and show us just how powerful we really are. No matter how dire circumstances may seem, know you have the resources to overcome any problem. The tools introduced in this book can help guide the way.

THE POWER OF SHIFTING FOCUS

I learned this lesson firsthand from Louise Hay, the legendary founder of Hay House Publishing. Her wisdom didn't just inspire me—it fundamentally changed the way I approach challenges.

One evening, we were out to dinner, and I asked her a question that bothered me. "Louise, how do you handle hecklers in an audience?" As a public speaker, this was a real concern for me.

Her response was simple but profound: "Helene, when you see someone being discourteous in the audience, don't give them your energy. Instead, focus on the person engaged in what you're saying." Lee Glickstein, Founder of Speaking Circles International, confirmed Louise's wisdom.

That wasn't just advice for public speaking; it was a life philosophy. Louise taught me to focus on the positive, even in the face of negativity. Let's be honest: We live in a world where it's all too easy to dwell on what's wrong. But the real magic happens when we shift our attention to what's going right.

HOW POSITIVE IS YOUR ATTITUDE?

Take this quick quiz to see where your mindset currently stands. Be honest with yourself—awareness is the first step to transformation.

1. **First thing in the morning, when I wake up, I...**
   a. Look forward to the day.
   b. Feel attacked by negative thinking.
   c. Start my routine but wish I could go back to bed.
2. **When I meet a new person, I...**
   a. Am excited to learn about them.
   b. Don't trust them until they prove themselves.
   c. Feel neutral and lukewarm about the interaction.
3. **At work, I...**
   a. Look for new solutions and ways to grow.
   b. Watch the clock until 5 PM.
   c. Like my coworkers but feel stuck and unfulfilled in my job.
4. **My attitude toward people going the extra mile for me is...**
   a. I trust they'll come through.
   b. I believe they rarely deliver.
   c. I usually avoid asking for help because I'm unsure if I'd even get it.

Now, total your answers.

- Mostly **A's:** You have a positive outlook and will likely thrive in different areas of life.

- Mostly **B's:** Negativity may dominate your mindset, holding you back from reaching your potential.
- Mostly **C's:** You feel conflicted, caught between hope and doubt.

Wherever you fall on the spectrum, know this: your mindset isn't fixed. It can be reshaped.

THE CALL TO CHANGE

You didn't pick up this book by accident. Maybe you're fed up with living a life that feels limited. Maybe you've been chasing growth but are disappointed with the results, wondering why fulfillment is still out of reach.

Here's the truth: They say that *when the student is ready, the teacher appears* and you are ready now because you are diving into this book and doing its exercises.

THE THREE C'S IN ACTION

The following stories are of people who turned their lives around under extraordinary circumstances. Their situations may seem extreme, but the steps they followed—clarity, commitment, and continuous action—are universal.

Clarity

Each started by clarifying their real problem. Clarity is about cutting through the noise of excuses, distractions, and blame to see the root of the issue.

Commitment

Once they understood their problem, they committed to change. This wasn't about half-hearted attempts—it was a full-on declaration to themselves and the world that they were ready to act.

Continuous Action

Transformation doesn't happen overnight. It requires consistent, focused effort. These individuals didn't stop after one success; they kept going, adjusting and evolving as they moved forward.

TRANSFORMATION THROUGH ADVERSITY: STORIES OF GROWTH AND REDEMPTION

Adversity, when faced with courage and honesty, can be the catalyst for profound transformation. Elsa, Kendall, and Charlie confronted their struggles, found clarity, and began living a more abundant life. Each journey is unique, yet they share a common thread: a moment of truth that sparked change and the commitment to act despite fear or doubt. Let their examples remind you of what's possible.

ELSA: SHEDDING THE WEIGHT OF SELF-DECEPTION

Elsa was carrying fifty extra pounds, but the burden wasn't just physical; it was also emotional. She wore colorful tent dresses and makeup, acting as if she were thin, trying to project an image that didn't align with her reality. While she managed to maintain her job and some friendships, she was weighed down by a persistent, low-grade depression.

Her wake-up call came at an unexpected moment. Stepping out of a swimming pool, Elsa caught her reflection in the glass door. She could no longer deny the truth staring back at her. But acknowledging the problem wasn't enough. Frustrated and overwhelmed, she overindulged for a week, stuck in a cycle of self-sabotage.

A friend who was concerned about her called to recommend a new weight-loss group. Despite her doubts, Elsa decided to give it a try. The group welcomed her with laughter, honesty, and a sense of community. That connection gave her the courage to keep going. Today, Elsa has lost fifteen pounds and remains committed to her transformational journey.

Living Richly Practice
Come Clean!

What are you pretending isn't important, but deep down, you know it is? Is it holding you back from experiencing life more fully? Take a few days to reflect on this. Write down your observations and share them with a trusted friend or advisor.

KENDALL: TURNING PAIN INTO STRENGTH

Raised by an abusive uncle, Kendall's childhood was filled with fear and instability. When he wasn't on long-haul trucking trips, his unpredictable temper left her constantly on edge. Her cousin offered some solace, but Kendall learned early on to be independent and fend for herself, which later proved valuable in her career.

Despite her challenging upbringing, Kendall broke barriers in her family, becoming the first to graduate from college. Today, she's a successful supervisor at a consumer goods company. Yet, unresolved trauma began surfacing in the form of panic attacks. Encouraged by her cousin, Kendall sought therapy, where she faced the truth about her past and the scars it left on her relationships.

Through treatment, Kendall began forgiving her uncle and, more importantly, herself. She's now developing a few quality friendships and working towards a fuller, richer life.

CHARLIE: FROM LOSS TO A LIFE OF PURPOSE

Charlie grew up in a wealthy family, inheriting millions when his father passed away. Financial security meant he could pursue his passion for acting. Charlie married a wonderful woman, and together, they built a life with two children on a rural farm.

But Charlie had a gambling addiction. Within three years, the inheritance was gone. Tragedy struck when a faulty heater caused a fire that destroyed their home. Devastated, he and his family turned to a local church for help.

The community rallied, providing temporary housing, food, and necessities. The church's Reverend encouraged Charlie to address his gambling problem, and he joined a recovery group. With newfound resolve, Charlie studied for his real estate license. Today, he's a successful agent in a nearby town, helping families find homes.

Charlie's belief in God and the support of his community carried him through a dark period. Reflecting on his journey, he says, "The money I inherited didn't mean as much as the paycheck I collect now. I feel like I'm truly making a difference in people's lives."

DECLUTTERING YOUR LIFE TO LIVE RICHLY

Living Richly isn't just about money or career success—it's about creating physical, emotional, and mental space for what truly matters. Ina and Maria's stories illustrate how clearing the clutter, whether physical possessions or poor habits, can create room for abundance and fulfillment.

WHEN SHE LET GO OF CLUTTER, HER LIFE EXPANDED

Ina's home was filled with old clothes, broken appliances, and unused items. Her clutter wasn't just physical—it symbolized the emotional weight she carried.

Her wake-up call came when her sister Lila visited and gently confronted her. Lila's honesty and support led Ina to seek professional help with her problem. Together, Lila and Ina worked to clear the house. As the physical clutter disappeared, the emotional burden began to heal. With the help of her therapist, Ina's life began to expand. She started going out and creating space for new friendships.

Clutter isn't just about the things we own; it's about what we're holding onto emotionally. When we let go of the unnecessary, we make room for what truly matters.

Living Richly Practice
Streamlining Your Space

• Choose one area—a desk, a closet, or a counter.

• Set a timer for 15 minutes and begin decluttering. Limiting the time helps reduce feeling overwhelmed.

• Repeat this daily for a week. Notice how good it feels to make progress.

• Find a decluttering buddy to keep each other accountable and celebrate your wins!

SHE TOOK CONTROL OF HER TIME AND STOPPED UNDEREARNING

Maria had a big heart, but her relationship with money was holding her back. Growing up, she internalized the belief that "money is the root of all evil." She undervalued her services and gave them away for free, barely able to support herself.

Time management was another struggle. Maria couldn't say no to favors, constantly overcommitting and feeling overwhelmed.

Her breakthrough came when she joined a 12-week financial wellness program in her community. She started to realize the monetary value of her time and the importance of setting boundaries. She began prioritizing income-producing activities and saying "no" to requests that didn't align with her goals.

Maria's transformation didn't stop at the course. She joined a small group that met weekly to reinforce the lessons she learned. A year later, Maria's earnings increased, and she had more time for self-care and for her loved ones.

Her story reminds us that time is our most precious commodity. When we use it wisely, we are more fulfilled.

Living Richly Practice
Reclaiming Your Time

Reflect on how you're spending your time each day. Ask yourself:

1. Am I prioritizing income-producing activities? List the tasks that directly contribute to your financial growth.

2. Am I carving out time for self-care? Schedule activities that recharge your energy.

3. Am I spending quality time with the people who matter most? Identify ways to connect more deeply with loved ones.

4. What feels out of balance? What surprises you about how you allocate your time?

FINDING A BALANCE AND MOVING FORWARD: TIME AS YOUR RICHEST RESOURCE

Living Richly isn't just about what you achieve; it's about how you spend your most valuable commodity: time. Without good management, it's easy to feel drained, overworked, or disconnected from what truly matters. This chapter emphasizes the power of clarity, commitment, and continuous action (the three C's). They can help you realign your priorities and advance with purpose.

FINDING HARMONY AND FULFILLMENT:

ADJUSTING TIME IMBALANCE

SELF-CARE
HEALTH, REST
REFLECTION

_____ %

$
INCOME
PRODUCING
ACTIONS

_____ %

FAMILY /
FRIENDS
QUALITY TIME,
CONNECTION

_____ %

FINDING HARMONY AND FULFILLMENT: ADJUSTING TIME IMBALANCE

Indicate how you would like your time to be distributed by assigning a percentage to each circle: Self-Care, Income-Producing Actions, and Family/Friends.

Living Richly Practice
Making Changes

---

1. Identify the changes needed to make your ideal time distribution a reality.

2. Set one concrete goal for each category (e.g., schedule weekly family dinners, take a 20-minute walk daily for self-care).

3. Share your plan with a trusted friend, coach, or mentor to help you stay accountable and take actionable steps.

ASKING FOR HELP IS A SIGN OF STRENGTH

Change begins when we're willing to reach out for help. Every transformational story in this book shares that common thread. Despite what many believe, asking for help isn't a weakness—it's a bold, powerful move toward growth.

Do any of these resonate with you?

- Reaching out to a mentor for career guidance.
- Asking a neighbor to step in for a childcare emergency.
- Confiding in a friend about an emotionally challenging situation and feeling the weight lift as they listen.

Think about the support you have around you. Sometimes, the hardest part is simply asking, but the results can be life-changing. Support isn't just about solving problems; it's about knowing you're not alone on the journey.

CHAPTER TAKEAWAYS

- **Clutter Limits Growth:** Whether it's physical possessions or emotional baggage, holding on to unnecessary things keeps us stuck.
- **Boundaries Create Abundance:** Saying "no" to what doesn't serve you allows you to say "yes" to what does.
- **Time is Power:** When you manage your time intentionally, you create space for more prosperity and joy instead of feeling drained, overworked, and disconnected.
- **Support is Key:** Whether it's a financial wellness program, a decluttering buddy, or a trusted confidant, having support accelerates your growth.

NUGGET FROM THE HEART

Have faith in yourself and the life you're creating. Even in the most challenging moments, there's always a lesson, a silver lining, or an opportunity to grow.

FOR YOUR JOURNAL

1. Are you often too exhausted at the end of the day, unable to spend quality time with the people you care about? If so, how can you stop repeating that negative pattern?
2. Are you sometimes too proud to ask for help when you need it? What is the price you pay for not asking for support?

CHAPTER 14

⚜

DISCIPLINE IS YOUR FRIEND

The thing we resist the most often becomes our greatest ally.

*L*et's face it: discipline gets a bad rap. We associate it with rigid rules, punishment, and authority figures telling us what we can't do. But what if we reframe discipline as a superpower that enables us to follow through, act, and get closer to our dreams?

Discipline isn't about restriction; it's about empowerment. It's the structure that allows you to stay focused, maintain peace of mind, and achieve results. Without it, distractions, excuses, and chaos take over.

REDEFINING DISCIPLINE: A NEW PERSPECTIVE

Think of discipline as the routine that supports your growth. It's the daily habits that keep you grounded and the mindset that keeps you focused. When you have discipline in place, you create a foundation for success in every area of life.

For example, if you allow distractions or negative thoughts to derail you, your energy will be drained, and nothing meaningful will happen. But with discipline, you can quiet the noise, focus on what matters, and confidently move forward.

HOW DISCIPLINED ARE YOU?

Take the following quiz to assess your relationship with discipline.

1. **When you start your day, you...**
   a. Follow a routine that energizes you.
   b. Hit the snooze button and wish for more sleep.
   c. Get up but feel unmotivated.
2. **When distractions arise at work, you...**
   a. Refocus on your tasks and keep going.
   b. Get caught up in conversations or gossip.
   c. Acknowledge the distraction but struggle to get back on track.
3. **At a restaurant, you...**
   a. Make healthy choices and feel good about them.
   b. Indulge in unhealthy options and regret it later.
   c. Try to eat healthily but give in to temptation halfway through.
4. **When your friend invites you out, but you've made another commitment, you...**
   a. Politely decline and make plans for another time.
   b. Try to do both, and overcommit.
   c. Cancel one plan and feel conflicted about it.

Results:

- Mostly **A's**: You've got a strong handle on discipline and use it to stay on track.
- Mostly **B's**: You struggle with discipline and may feel the effects of being disorganized or distracted.
- Mostly **C's**: You're conflicted about discipline—part of you sees its value, but you resist fully committing.

THE PITFALLS OF A LACK OF DISCIPLINE

Without discipline, it's easy to fall into common traps:

- **Lack of focus:** Getting derailed by distractions.
- **Procrastination:** Struggling to take the first step.
- **Overthinking:** Obsessing over details and nothing gets done.
- **Sloppiness:** Misplacing important information or forgetting tasks.
- **Perfectionism:** Setting impossible standards that lead to paralysis.

Discipline is the antidote to these challenges. It involves organization, prioritization, and creating habits that support one's goals.

DISCIPLINE IN ACTION: EVERYDAY EXAMPLES

Lack of Discipline:

> Your child is upset, but she's safe with a trusted babysitter. Yet you can't focus at work because you're consumed with worry.

Using Discipline:

> You remind yourself of the facts—your babysitter is reliable, and your child is fine. You refocus on the work at hand.

Lack of Discipline:

> You're hosting a dinner party, and the bakery fails to deliver the dessert as promised. You panic, convinced the evening is ruined.

Using Discipline:

> You take a breath and think of solutions. You call a family member to pick up a dessert or whip up something simple yourself. Problem solved.

CREATING A DAILY ROUTINE FOR SUCCESS

A disciplined routine isn't about being rigid; it's about setting yourself up for success. My own routine includes prayer, meditation, and a quick morning check-in with an accountability partner. These simple practices help me prioritize what matters most and stay on track throughout the day.

1. Morning Prayer: Start with Gratitude

The moment we wake up, our minds often flood us with worries, doubts, or a never-ending to-do list. This Mad Mind-Chatter can set the tone for your entire day if you let it. That's why I counteract it immediately with prayer—a practice that centers me and brings clarity. It's the perfect way to ground myself in gratitude for the day ahead.

Try this:

> *"Thank you, God, for the unexpected blessings You are sending me now. I greet this day with positive expectations about the people I will meet and the opportunities before me."*

This simple practice has a calming effect on me, no matter what challenges lie ahead.

SHERRY'S STORY: LEANING ON PRAYER IN HARD TIMES

Sherry, a close friend of mine, works in human resources for a large corporation. During the height of COVID-19, her workload doubled, and she experienced the loss of her beloved brother Jim to cancer. Exhausted and grieving, Sherry found solace in her daily prayer practice. Every morning, she reads something inspirational and prays for the strength to face the day ahead. She often says, "God takes care of those who pray."

2. Repetitive Chant: Rewire Your Mindset

Even after prayer, my mind can go back to fear or doubt. That's when I rely on a repetitive chant to reinforce positive energy.

Try this:

"I have the time and energy to accomplish the tasks before me with grace and ease."

Say it a few times, briskly and with intention. This chant reminds you that you're in control of your day, not the other way around.

3. Quick Exercise: Energize Your Body and Mind

Nothing boosts your mood like movement. Whether it's a 15-minute walk, a quick yoga session, or jumping jacks, the key is to get moving.

"I'm fortunate to live in a building with a swimming pool, so I start my day with water aerobics."

4. Meditation: Finding Peace in Stillness

After breakfast, I meditate for 20 minutes. If meditation is new to you, start with just five minutes a day and build from there. You can find guided meditations on YouTube or simply sit quietly, focusing on your breath.

GRETTA'S STORY: FINDING PEACE AND FRIENDSHIP

Gretta, a friend of mine, rediscovered the power of meditation after moving to a new state for work. Lonely and struggling to adjust, she took her mother's advice and restarted her practice. One evening, after meditating, she had the idea to visit a local restaurant where she discovered a karaoke group and joined in. That chance encounter led to a weekly tradition and new friendships.

Meditation isn't just about relaxation—it opens your mind to creative solutions and unexpected opportunities.

5. Action Buddy: Accountability Leads to Success

An action buddy can be a game-changer. You connect with this person daily to share your goals and hold each other accountable. The exchange is simple and powerful:

- One person takes five minutes to share their daily actions.
- The other gives two minutes of feedback.
- Then, you switch roles.

These short calls provide clarity, motivation, and a sense of partnership.

GEORGE'S STORY: TURNING FEAR INTO ACTION

George, an acquaintance of mine, was downsized from his job as a store manager. Feeling paralyzed by fear and inertia, he struggled to move forward with a new business he had started with friends. I suggested he find an action buddy to keep him accountable.

He partnered with a woman facing similar career challenges. Together, they held daily check-ins, providing support and feedback. Recently, George told me how transformative this practice has been for both of them.

Living Richly Practice
Building Your Morning Routine

If you don't have a morning routine, here's how to start your day with clarity and purpose:

1. Prayer: Begin with gratitude to set a positive tone.

2. Chant: Use a repetitive phrase to reinforce your focus.

3. Exercise: Move your body to boost energy and mood.

4. Meditation: Create space for reflection and inspiration.

5. Action Buddy: Share your daily goals and get feedback.

WHY THESE PRACTICES MATTER

These habits aren't just about checking boxes; they're about creating a foundation for success. When you start your day with intention, you set the stage for meaningful action and personal growth.

HOW DISCIPLINED ARE YOU WITH YOUR TIME?

As I said in the last chapter, time is the most precious resource we have, yet many of us feel as if there is never enough of it. In fact, in the Smart Women Live Richly Survey, 68% of our respondents said that they could do better and be more efficient with their time.

Do you ever find yourself wondering where your day went? Are you "time-drunk," wasting hours without even realizing it? Take this quiz to find out.

QUIZ: HOW TIME-EFFICIENT ARE YOU?

1. **You have several chores that must be done before leaving home. You...**
   a. Do them one by one.
   b. Get distracted by a TV program and do none of them.
   c. Try to multitask but finish only one chore.

2. **Your friend hates it when you're late for lunch. You...**
   a. Make an extra effort to be on time.
   b. Show up 15 minutes late.
   c. Try to be on time but still end up late.

3. **Your boss shifts priorities and asks for a report by 5:00 p.m. You...**
   a. Drop what you're doing and complete the report on time.
   b. Don't shift your tasks and miss the deadline.
   c. Work on both tasks, finishing neither properly.

4. **At the end of the day, you feel unproductive. You...**
   a. Check your to-do list to see if you have completed three key tasks and give yourself credit for doing them.
   b. Shame yourself for not finishing the most important task.
   c. Express disappointment that you didn't do everything on your list, but acknowledge that you did finish one of your priorities.

Results:

- Mostly **A's**: You're efficient with your time and likely have solid routines in place.
- Mostly **B's**: Time often slips through your fingers. Awareness and discipline can help.
- Mostly **C's**: You're conflicted about the way you use your time but show potential to improve.

DISCIPLINE, TIME, AND POWER

Your time management reflects your priorities. Discipline helps you align your actions with what matters most. Whether on high-impact tasks or letting go of distractions, your commitment to using time wisely will transform your life.

STORIES OF DISCIPLINE IN ACTION

Sherry: Overcoming Worry with a Special Routine

Sherry worried about her teenage daughter's struggles at school. Her anxiety consumed her nights, leaving her exhausted during the day. She learned to implement a nightly prayer routine, releasing her worries and focusing on what she could do to support her daughter. This simple shift helped her sleep better and be more present for her family.

Gerald: Prioritizing Income-Producing Tasks

Gerald ran a small business but spent most of the mornings buried in emails and organizing files. His revenue started to increase once he shifted his mornings to focus on sales calls and client outreach.

TIME RAIDER VS. DISCIPLINE SHIFT

Every day, we face choices that either steal our time or help us use it wisely. Let's explore some of these contrasting behaviors.

1. **Time Raiders: Focusing on others' unsolvable problems.**
   - You waste time worrying about things you can't control.
   - **Discipline Shift:** Help as much as possible, then move on to what you can control.
2. **Overloading your to-do list.**
   - Trying to tackle ten tasks when you can only handle five leads to exhaustion and inefficiency.
   - **Discipline Shift:** Set realistic priorities and save the rest for tomorrow.
3. **Overthinking.**

- You lose sleep trying to find a solution to a problem beyond your control.
- **Discipline Shift:** Pray, or meditate, and know a solution will present itself at the right time.

4. **Focusing on low-value tasks.**
   - Spending mornings on admin work instead of income-generating activities.
   - **Discipline Shift:** Handle your most important tasks first thing in the morning.

Managing your time and keeping discipline in the forefront sets you up to take smart risks. The next chapter will explore how stepping out of your comfort zone can help you push past limits and unlock opportunities.

CHAPTER TAKEAWAYS

- Without discipline, you are prone to procrastination and a lack of focus on what is important.
- A daily routine that includes prayer, exercise, and setting clear priorities leads to success.
- Discipline is key to using your time efficiently and achieving your goals.
- Identify your "time raiders" and replace them with "discipline shifts."

NUGGET FROM THE HEART

Time management is power. It's essential for creating the life you deserve.

FOR YOUR JOURNAL

1. How has being disciplined helped you move forward in your life?
2. Do you have a morning routine? If not, what steps will you take to create one?

CHAPTER 15

⚜

TAKING CALCULATED RISKS

Living a life beyond one's wildest dreams is possible for those who dare to step out of their comfort zone and take Smart Risks.

Smart risk-taking involves courage, commitment, and a willingness to leap toward what you want most. It's about embracing unknown territory and forging meaningful connections that elevate not only your life but also the lives of others.

THE POWER OF TAKING RISKS

Living Richly is about more than comfort; it's about impact. Your insights, actions, and courage to take risks can spark change in ways you may not even imagine. But how often do we hold ourselves back, fearing failure, rejection or judgment? The truth is, stepping outside of your comfort zone isn't just an option; it's a requirement for growth.

Taking risks isn't about recklessness; it's about calculated, intentional actions. But first, let's see where you stand when it comes to creating impact.

QUIZ: ARE YOU HAVING THE IMPACT YOU WANT?

1. **At work, you have an idea to solve a problem your team is stuck on. You...**
   a. Offer the idea to the team.
   b. Stay silent, assuming your co-workers won't take you seriously.
   c. Wait for the "perfect time" to speak up, which never comes.

2. **At a Parent/Teacher night, the principal asks for suggestions. You...**
   a. Share an idea to raise funds for athletic equipment.
   b. Let others speak while you keep quiet.
   c. Want to contribute but doubt your ability to make a difference, so you stay silent.

3. **You're frustrated about the upcoming election. You...**
   a. Volunteer for the campaign of the candidate you endorse.
   b. Complain about the candidates but take no action.
   c. Feel too busy to help, even though you want to get involved.

4. **Your son seems distant and depressed. You...**
   a. Sit down with him, express your concern, and offer your support.
   b. Assume he's just moody and wouldn't accept your help anyway.
   c. Worry but feel unsure about how to approach him, so you do nothing.

Results:

- Mostly **A's**: You take action and are likely to have a positive impact on those around you.
- Mostly **B's**: You may feel disengaged or hesitant to take action, which limits your influence.
- Mostly **C's**: You're conflicted about how to step up and create meaningful change.

What patterns do you notice in your answers? If you're not making the impact you'd like, know this: You can. Your unwillingness to act and face potential discomfort may be holding you back.

THE COURAGE TO STEP OUT OF YOUR COMFORT ZONE

Our greatest loss comes from holding back ideas or actions out of fear of judgment. Every time you suppress your voice, you deny yourself the opportunity to grow and evolve.

Look at the incredible work of Malala Yousafzai, who risked everything to fight for girls' education. Her courage reminds us that even one voice can create ripples of change.

When I founded Creative Expansions, Inc., my mission was to empower women and girls globally. I envisioned a pebble dropped into water, creating concentric circles. That pebble symbolized one woman speaking up, while the ripples represented the people inspired by her courage. Today, that vision has touched millions of lives, proving that stepping out of your comfort zone can create an impact far beyond what you initially imagined.

THE DIFFERENCE BETWEEN RECKLESS AND CALCULATED RISKS

Taking risks doesn't mean acting without thought—it's about making informed, purposeful decisions that challenge your limits while focusing on your goals.

Let's break it down:

RECKLESS RISKS

- Quitting your job impulsively without a backup plan.
- Investing money you can't afford to lose in a high-risk venture.
- Saying yes to opportunities that don't align with your values or goals.

CALCULATED RISKS

- Leaving a job after securing another opportunity or creating a financial safety net.
- Doing your own research and consulting experts before making a major investment.
- Stepping up to lead a project at work, even if it scares you, because it aligns with your long-term career vision.

WHY CALCULATED RISKS MATTER

Every great achievement starts with someone daring to take a risk. It's about looking fear in the face and stepping forward anyway. You might fail, but even failure teaches you valuable lessons.

Taking calculated risks can strengthen resilience and broaden your capacity to *Live Richly*.

Living Richly Practice
Let Your Voice Be Heard

Don't hold back when you know the answer to a problem or have an idea that could make a difference. Mad Mind-Chatter may try to convince you that you'll look foolish, but that's fear talking. Ignore it. *Living Richly* is about using your unique talents to impact the lives of others.

THE POWER OF STEPPING OUTSIDE YOUR COMFORT ZONE

Imagine this: You're in a room you know well, but the lights are off. Suddenly, the familiar becomes disorienting. You take a deep breath, blink your eyes in the darkness, and rely on memory, logic, and intuition to navigate. Each careful step gets you closer to the door, the exit, and the opportunity waiting beyond it.

This is what it feels like to take a smart risk. The path is uncertain, but you move forward with calculated steps and trust in your abilities. Life often calls on us to navigate unfamiliar territory, to risk failure or rejection for the sake of something greater.

The key is discernment. How do you determine which risks are worth taking? That's where the concept of a *smart risk* comes in.

SMART RISKS: A METHOD FOR DECISION-MAKING

To decide if a risk is worth taking, follow these four steps:

1. Analyze the Pluses and Minuses. Draw a line down the middle of a page. Write the potential benefits on one side and the potential downsides on the other. Which list is longer?

2. Assess the Timing. Consider where you are in your life and whether this is the right moment for this particular leap. Ask yourself:

- Are you just **starting out** (single, early in your career, or exploring possibilities)?
- Are you in the **established phase** (raising children, climbing the corporate ladder, or juggling multiple responsibilities)?
- Are you in your **second or third act** (adjusting to an empty nest, caregiving, or focusing on legacy and purpose)?

Timing is crucial. Even a great opportunity may not align with your current stage of life.

3. Align with Core Values. Ask yourself: Will achieving this goal honor my core values or create conflict? *Living Richly* means staying true to who you are.

4. Trust Your Gut. What is your intuition telling you? Sometimes, your gut provides clarity that logic alone cannot. If you feel an undeniable pull toward something, that's worth listening to.

When your analysis, timing, values, and intuition align, that's what I call a **"best bet."** If the timing feels off, it might be a **"not now."** And if something conflicts with your values or doesn't sit right, it's a **"no go."**

TAKING RISKS FOR A RICHER LIFE

Don't shy away from a "best bet." Stepping out of your comfort zone is never easy. The fear of failure is real, but so is the potential for growth, impact, and fulfillment. Each calculated risk brings you closer to *Living Richly*, allowing you to expand your horizons and achieve what once seemed impossible.

Living Richly Practice
Analyze a Risk That's Timely

---

1. Identify a risk you're considering taking in your life right now.

2. Write down the pluses and minuses in two columns.

3. Reflect on the timing: Is now the right moment, or should you wait?

4. Connect with your values: Does this align with what matters most to you?

5. Listen to your intuition: What is your gut telling you?

If the answers align, take the leap. If they don't, it might mean the timing isn't right—or that it never will be.

Living Richly means embracing the discomfort of the unknown to pursue a bigger, bolder vision for your life. You can navigate the darkness, trust your inner compass, and step into the light of new opportunities. Let's look at how Dale, Cynthia, Samantha, and Abby used the smart risk method to determine if their risks were "best bets."

SMART RISK METHOD IN ACTION

Dale: Moving for Career Growth

Dale grew up in Puerto Rico in a close-knit family. After excelling in school, she moved to New York City for college and later secured an entry-level position at a major financial institution. Her hard work and charisma quickly paid off—within two years, she was offered a substantial promotion at another company in a different state.

This opportunity came with challenges: relocating, learning new skills quickly, and uprooting her life in New York. But Dale used the Smart Risk Method. She listed her pros and cons, found that the advantages outweighed the disadvantages, and confirmed that the company's values aligned with her own. The timing was perfect; no family obligations held her back. Confident in her analysis, she took the leap, paving the way for a brighter future.

Cynthia: Balancing Duty and Dreams

Widowed with grown children, Cynthia was nearing retirement and eager to fulfill her dream of traveling. She won an all-expenses-paid trip to Africa to witness the Great Migration, a once-in-a-lifetime opportunity. But her sister, who was ill, needed her help.

Conflicted, Cynthia used the Smart Risk Method to make her decision. While the trip aligned with her core values and was perfectly timed for her life stage, her sister's health was a major concern. After consulting with the doctor and enlisting her children to assist with caregiving, she gave herself permission to go. Cynthia's courage to trust in support systems allowed her to live out her dream while ensuring her sister was cared for.

Samantha: Making a Choice When Life Gets Complicated

Samantha, a single mother, was presented with a life-changing decision. Her boyfriend, John, had been offered a prestigious job in Switzerland and wanted Samantha and her children to join him. While he offered financial security and proposed marriage, she hesitated.

Her Smart Risk analysis revealed a complex situation. The opportunity was exciting but involved uprooting her children from their school and friends. Though she cared for John, her feelings about marriage weren't definitive. With her pros and cons nearly equal, Samantha realized the timing wasn't right. She and John decided to maintain their relationship long-distance, giving them both time to reassess their future.

Abby: Finding New Challenges

Abby, a beauty consultant for ten years, felt stuck in her career. When pressed about her dreams, she admitted she wanted to be a screenwriter. Her local college offered a summer course in screenwriting, conveniently located near her salon.

Abby used the Smart Risk Method to evaluate this step. The pros were clear: pursuing a long-held dream and expanding her creative horizons. The cons were minimal since she could keep her job while taking the course. She registered for the class, starting her journey conservatively but with purpose. By taking this small but meaningful step, Abby opened a door to new possibilities without overwhelming herself.

REFLECT AND ACT: SHIFT IMBALANCES

Imbalances in work, relationships, and personal time can prevent us from *Living Richly*. You're not alone if you've felt overwhelmed by responsibilities, stuck in routines, or unfulfilled in your personal or professional life. But you don't have to stay stuck. By recognizing these patterns and taking calculated actions which can feel risky, you are able to move toward a more fulfilled and abundant life.

Now it's your turn. Reflect on the following examples. Do you identify with any of them?

WORK: TOO-MUCH-WORK IMBALANCE

Casey's demanding day job had her on call at night. Though she shared childcare responsibilities with her husband, her mind was constantly on work, leaving her little energy for the family. The stress even started manifesting physically, with heart palpitations. Casey needed to set boundaries before burnout consumed her.

Do you sometimes feel indispensable at work, putting in longer hours than necessary? Do your family and friends feel neglected because your mind is elsewhere when you are with them? If so, you might be experiencing the too-much-work imbalance.

Calculated Actions to Take:

1. **Set Boundaries:** Establish a "cut-off time" for work each day and stick to it. Use this time to reconnect with your family or enjoy personal downtime.
2. **Plan a Break:** Schedule a mini-vacation or day trip to a new destination. Make it a non-negotiable commitment.
3. **Morning Quiet Time:** Take 10 minutes in the morning to reflect, breathe, and set priorities for the day.

WORK: VOCATIONAL-MALAISE IMBALANCE

Denice felt trapped in a job that used only half of her skills. Although she stayed because of its stability, deep down, she yearned for work that challenged her and made her feel valued.

Do you feel underutilized in your current job? Are you staying put out of fear of the unknown? This imbalance can leave you feeling stagnant and unfulfilled.

Calculated Actions to Take:

1. **Define Your Goals:** Write down specific career objectives. If you're uncertain, seek the guidance of a career coach.
2. **Find Inspiration:** Talk to people who love their jobs and use their experiences to spark ideas.
3. **Follow Your Intuition:** Trust any "wild hunches" or creative ideas—they could lead to unexpected opportunities.
4. **Network:** Expand your professional circle. Let people know you're open to new challenges and ready for more responsibility.

FAMILY: NO-SPECIAL-SOMEONE-TO-LOVE IMBALANCE

Marnie lost her husband seven years ago and had not ventured into the dating world since. Her loneliness became overwhelming, but fear of the unknown held her back.

Are you single and yearning for connection but too scared to take action? If this resonates, it's time to step outside your comfort zone.

Calculated Actions to Take:

- **Stay Engaged:** Keep doing the activities you love and remain open to meeting new people.
- **Define Your Ideal Relationship:** Make a list of qualities you want in a partner and what you can bring to the table.
- **Leverage Your Network:** Let your friends know you're ready to meet someone special—they may have introductions in mind.

FRIENDS: SAME-OLD-ROUTINE IMBALANCE

Rosa loved her friends, but their predictable routines left her feeling uninspired. She craved adventure and spontaneity but didn't know where to start.

Do you feel stuck in a rut socially? Do you crave more excitement in your friendships? If so, it's time to shake things up.

Calculated Actions to Take:

1. **Try Something New:** Attend an event, workshop, or party, and invite your friends along. Push yourself to take phone numbers from new people and stay connected.
2. **Revisit Old Passions:** Think of an activity you used to love but haven't done in a while—and start doing it again. Invite your friends to come along, but if they don't want to go, you go!
3. **Reconnect:** Reach out to someone you care about but haven't seen in a while. Plan something fun and out of the ordinary to do together.

ME: LITTLE TIME FOR SELF-CARE IMBALANCE

For many people, including me, self-care can be pushed aside if there is a work or family emergency. But self-care is not a luxury; it is necessary. It is how we recharge our batteries and avoid burnout. When another person's demands bombard us (mind you, there is really no emergency), do we say "no," or do we acquiesce?

Calculated Actions to Take:

1. **Prioritize Quiet Time:** Spend at least 10 minutes daily reflecting or meditating. Use this time to recharge.
2. **Start Small:** Schedule one act of self-care, like taking a walk, reading a book, or enjoying a long bath. Make sure to pencil it in on your calendar.
3. **Draw a Boundary:** Say "no" to a request that conflicts with your "me time" unless there really is an emergency.

Living Richly Practice
Action Plan

To address these imbalances, create a plan and hold yourself accountable.

1. Identify an Imbalance: Choose one area where you feel stuck.

2. Take Action: Select two to three actionable steps from the suggestions given for countering the imbalances.

3. Set a Timeline: Write down specific dates for taking these steps.

4. Find Accountability: Share your plan with a trusted friend or mentor to stay on track.

Changing habits isn't easy and can feel risky. In fact, the fear of the unknown may tempt us to hold on, rather than let go and try something new.

LETTING GO VS. HOLDING ON

Letting go is a risk worth taking. When you step into the unknown with faith and courage, life often meets you halfway. Holding on, meanwhile, keeps us stuck in unhealthy patterns. Here's how these choices can shape your life.

Holding On:

> You remain in a dead-end job, rationalizing, "At least I'm earning a paycheck."

Letting Go:

> You recognize that your current position no longer challenges or fulfills you. You contact a career coach, update your resume, and begin networking for opportunities.

Holding On:

> A close friend moves across the country for a promotion, and your thoughts center on how much you'll miss her rather than celebrating her success.

Letting Go:

> You acknowledge your sadness but focus on her happiness. You plan a visit and stay connected through regular calls or video chats. You have faith that you can build other close relationships.

Holding On:

> You remain in a toxic relationship out of fear of being single or starting over.

Letting Go:

> You prioritize your well-being and decide to move on, trusting that a healthier relationship and new opportunities will arise when you create space for it.

AVA'S STORY: LETTING GO OF A TOXIC MARRIAGE

Ava, in her early forties with a young child, faced the end of her marriage after years of couples counseling. Though she feared the financial and emotional toll of separation, she also knew the constant tension was unhealthy for her family. A friend and mentor encouraged her to leave by saying, "When you let go of this relationship, you'll free up energy for better things to come into your life." Ava was skeptical but took the leap—and her friend was right. Within a year, Ava was given more responsibility at her job, and her income increased. By letting go of what wasn't working, she made space for new opportunities.

BUILDING A SUPPORT NETWORK: "NO MATTER WHAT" FRIENDS AND MORE

Navigating risks and embracing change becomes easier with support from trustworthy friends, colleagues, mentors, and sponsors. These are the people who remind you of your potential and stand by you when fear or doubt creeps in.

SALLY'S STORY: FRIENDLY PERSUASION WORKS WONDERS

Sally dreamed of owning property but was overwhelmed by the financial and emotional demands of making it a reality. Her friend Charlotte introduced her to a real estate agent who knew of an affordable plot of land. Though Sally hesitated, daunted by the work involved in building a home, Charlotte's encouragement gave her the courage to move forward. Today, Sally owns the land and is ready to start construction.

Living Richly Practice
How to Grow Your Network

1. Identify the people in your life who inspire and support you, as well as those who might have extended themselves at one time and you never took them up on it.

2. Nurture these relationships by showing up for them as they do for you. Reach out to new contacts as well.

3. Don't hesitate to ask for help or advice when you need it, and reciprocate as well.

TAKING SMART RISKS WITH MENTORS AND SPONSORS

Living Richly means being willing to embrace change and take timely risks. These calculated risks involve thoughtful analysis, getting insights from trusted advisors, and the ability to handle uncertainty. Reaching out to work mentors and sponsors will help in this process.

THE ROLE OF WORK MENTORS

One of the most powerful relationships you can foster in your career is with a mentor. A mentor is someone who provides guidance, support, and encouragement while helping you navigate challenges and opportunities. But it's not just about what they can do for you—it's a mutual relationship that benefits both parties.

For example, Hannah, an ambitious professional, wanted to build a mentoring relationship with Raina, a supervisor from another department. After several unreturned calls, Hannah thought strategically: "What can I offer Raina?" She realized she could connect Raina with a key contact and family friend, the president of a local bank, who might be able to advance one of Raina's projects. Hannah's proactive approach sparked a mutually beneficial partnership with Raina.

Living Richly Practice
Actionable Steps to Find a Mentor

---

1. Identify someone whose career trajectory aligns with your goals.

2. Do the research—find your common interests and mutual contacts before approaching them.

3. Approach them with respect and offer something of value in return.

WORK SPONSORS: ELEVATING YOUR CAREER

Every type of relationship—whether between mentor and mentee or sponsor and sponsee—should be *mutually* beneficial.

While mentors provide guidance, sponsors are the leaders who can advocate for you when key decisions are made about promotions or special assignments. They will encourage you to take calculated risks that can advance your career.

Again, it's important that the relationship benefit both parties. For instance, a sponsor might highlight your achievements in a high-level meeting while you provide him or her with insights, contacts, or assistance on crucial projects. When approaching a potential sponsor, be clear about what you bring to the table.

Living Richly Practice
Steps to Approach a Sponsor

---

1. Identify influential leaders who can advocate for you.

2. Brainstorm ways you can add value to their work and where you would likely run into them.

3. When you connect with them, clearly communicate what you hope to achieve and how the relationship will benefit them.

CHAPTER TAKEAWAYS

- Taking calculated risks is essential for growth and fulfillment.
- You can evaluate risks using the framework of *Best Bet, Not Now, or No Go.*
- "No matter what" friends provide the support you need to navigate life's challenges.
- Mentorship and sponsorship are vital relationships for career and personal growth—and they should be mutually beneficial.

NUGGET FROM THE HEART

With effort, an open heart, and the support of others, you are poised to take Smart Risks that will lead you on an extraordinary journey of growth and abundance.

FOR YOUR JOURNAL

1. Reflect on a past risk you have taken. What was the outcome? How did it shape you?
2. What's a risk you know you should take but have been avoiding? Why?

3. If you don't have a mentor or sponsor at work, choose one of these relationships and outline the steps to create this connection. Who could you approach, and what value can you offer them in return?

THE SIXTH KEY

GROWING A GREATER LIFE

A prosperous life isn't just for the select few; it's your birthright. Greatness is within you, and the path to abundance begins with your decision to claim it.

CHAPTER 16

NINE TRUTHS TO LIVE BY

No one is just "lucky." Luck isn't found; it's created.

*P*rosperity isn't given; it's built. If your life isn't where you want it to be, you don't have to wait for permission to change it. Right now, at this very moment, you have the power to rewrite your story and take control of your destiny.

Living Richly isn't only about the amount of money in your bank account or the titles on your resume. It's about adopting a mindset that sees opportunities where others see obstacles, abundance where others see scarcity. Where you started doesn't matter—what matters is where you're headed. The life you want is waiting, but you must decide to step into it.

WHAT ARE THE NINE TRUTHS?

They're actionable principles designed to unlock a better life. They are not abstract theories. Let's dive in.

NUMBER 1: KINDNESS LIGHTS UP OUR LIVES

What you project will multiply and return to you. Kindness is a powerful force that transforms not just others but also you. One small act can create a ripple effect, spreading far beyond what you can see. Remember, negativity works the same way—it is your choice.

Kindness doesn't have to be grand. Smile at a stranger. Acknowledge someone's efforts. Empathize with a frustrated child and watch how the little one's energy shifts. The return on kindness is immeasurable.

NUMBER 2: YOU'RE CAPABLE OF MORE THAN YOU THINK

Whatever you believe you're capable of—double it, triple it. Why stop at a limited vision when you're built for limitless potential? The only thing standing in your way is the boundary you've created in your mind.

Take Cleo, for example. She came to me unsure of her direction, despite her brilliance. Through encouragement and clarity, she discovered her true passion. Unlike what her parents believed, it wasn't finance but advertising—a field where she's now thriving. You, too, can tap into hidden talents and achieve more than you've imagined.

NUMBER 3: PRAISE FUELS GROWTH

Think of praise as water to a parched garden. When you acknowledge someone's effort, you don't just lift their spirits; you energize their will to push forward. Be generous with your compliments. Notice the difference it makes not just in others but in the environment around them.

NUMBER 4: CONNECT WITH YOUR SOUL

Ever feel trapped by the noise in your mind? Your thoughts can be a storm, pulling you in every direction. The solution? Silence the chatter and reconnect with your essence.

Exercise: Stand before a mirror and look deeply into your eyes. It is said that the "eyes are the window to the soul." Now, reconnect with your inner wisdom about a challenge and ask for guidance. You'll be amazed at the clarity that emerges when you focus inward instead of outward.

NUMBER 5: SHARE YOUR STRUGGLES, SHARE YOUR STRENGTHS

Your pain isn't just a burden; it's a bridge. Every hardship you've endured equips you to help someone else.

I'll never forget the night I comforted a young woman devastated by the death of her mother. Sharing my own story and healing gave her hope in a moment of despair. Your challenges have value, not just for you but for others who need inspiration: "I've been there, and it will get easier."

NUMBER 6: NEVER GIVE UP—BUT TAKE A DAY OFF IF YOU MUST

Even the strongest of us need to regroup. Feeling frustrated or disheartened is okay, but only for a little while. Indulge the emotion, take a day off if needed, and then get back to work. Never give up on something you believe in.

Molly is an example of a talented musician who nearly quit her career after countless rejections. With encouragement from friends, she realized she had a calling—to heal others through her craft and kept going. Today, she's featured at events, and her audiences are uplifted by her performances. The lesson? Keep going. Your time will come.

NUMBER 7: TRUST YOUR GUT

Doubt isn't always your enemy; sometimes, it's your guide. If something feels off—a deal, a relationship, a decision—listen. Intuition is your internal compass, pointing you toward truth and away from trouble.

Think of those moments when your instincts screamed, "Something's wrong!" and you ignored them. Haven't we all been there? Learn to trust that inner voice. It rarely leads you astray.

NUMBER 8: DETACH FROM NEGATIVITY

The world is full of people who are struggling. Don't let their darkness cloud your light.

When faced with negativity, pause. Remind yourself: their behavior is about them, not you. Protect your energy, stay empathetic, and focus on the important work only you can do.

NUMBER 9: TIMING IS EVERYTHING

You cán't force the seasons, and you can't rush your journey. Plant your seeds, tend to them, and trust that they'll bloom when the time is right.

Claim Your Birthright

Prosperity isn't reserved for the lucky or privileged—it's available to anyone willing to believe, act, and grow.

Keep these truths in mind today, and watch your life transform in ways you never thought possible.

Living Richly Practice
Our Creed

Place your hand on your heart and say, out loud, the following:

Today, and every day going forward, I vow to Live Richly and express myself fully. Some days I may fall short, but when that happens, I will forgive myself and keep going.

THE QUALITIES OF LIVING RICHLY

You hold the keys to abundance, but as I have said throughout this book, maintaining a rich lifestyle isn't just about material wealth; it's about embodying the qualities that attract, grow, and sustain prosperity.

Look at the list below and reflect: Which qualities are part of your life now, and which ones do you need to incorporate?

- **The Ability to Focus On What You Want and Go After It**
  - Success follows clarity. Know what makes you come alive and take bold actions to get it.
- **The Ability to Have Fun**
  - Life is precious. Wear it like a loose garment, laugh often, and let joy lead the way.
- **The Ability to Respect Others' Differences**
  - True connection lies in embracing our differences. Appreciate what makes each person unique while celebrating your shared humanity.
- **The Ability to Prioritize and Let Go of the "Small Stuff"**
  - Life's too short to sweat the insignificant. Focus on what truly matters and use your time wisely.
- **The Ability to Give and Receive**
  - Prosperity flows when you are generous with your gifts and gracious when others offer theirs.
- **The Ability to Conserve Energy**
  - Burnout is the enemy of abundance. Pace yourself. Direct your energy where it counts most.
- **The Ability to Trust Your Inner Compass**
  - Confidence is knowing what's right for you, even when others disagree. Listen to your gut and trust the wisdom from within.
- **The Ability to Stay Positive, Even in Tough Times**
  - A positive outlook doesn't ignore challenges—it rises above them, creating space for solutions to emerge.
- **The Ability to Appreciate Life**
  - Every breath you take is a gift. Savor the present moment, and realize life's *little things* are really *big things*.
- **The Ability to Reach Out to Others in Need**
  - Prosperity thrives in connection. Empathy and support for others lead to inner harmony.
- **The Ability to Create a Vision for Your Life**

- Your life is a canvas. Dream boldly, then take deliberate action to create the masterpiece you envision.
- **The Ability to Ask for Help**
  - Pride can keep you isolated, but vulnerability builds bridges. Reach out and let others support you.

CHAPTER TAKEAWAYS

- Kindness has the power to transform lives.
- Praise reenergizes and fuels growth and connection.
- Intuition is an all-knowing guide—follow it.
- Protect your energy from negativity.
- Timing is everything; trust the process.

NUGGET FROM THE HEART

Don't let doubt rob you of your bounty. Dare to step into your greatness and prosper now.

FOR YOUR JOURNAL

1. Which one of the nine truths do you resonate with the most, and why?
2. Recall a time when sharing a painful experience helped someone else. How did it feel to use your hardship for good?
3. When the road gets tough and discouragement sets in, what strategies will you use to keep on track?

This chapter has been about adopting the qualities that will sustain *Living Richly*. Next, you'll discover how to let your unique brilliance shine and protect it from those who might try to dim its light.

CHAPTER 17

✍

SPARKLE, THE CURRENCY OF RICH LIVING

Sparkle is that radiant vitality that turns heads, lifts spirits,
and makes you the person others want to be around.

Sparkle isn't about perfection or pretense. It's the glow you emit when you're joyful, well-rested, and living in alignment with your best self.

When you're sparkling, you're irresistible. In a room full of stressed individuals, your energy becomes a lighthouse, drawing others toward you. But sparkle isn't a permanent fixture; it's a flame that must be nurtured. Lose sight of your well-being, and it will dim.

WHO TOOK MY SPARKLE?

I know this firsthand. Years ago, I found myself running on empty—exhausted, overextended, and, frankly, burned out. I wrote a book with a rough title, *Who Took My Sparkle?* But the truth is, I already knew the answer: *me*.

It wasn't an easy realization. I had prioritized everything and everyone else over my own needs. It wasn't until a long weekend at a yoga retreat—

walking through serene woods, swimming in a tranquil lake—that I saw clearly: I had been my own sparkle thief. The only person who could restore it was me.

WHAT DIMS YOUR SPARKLE?

It's not just burnout caused by overextending yourself that dims our sparkle. Other people can play a role too—whether intentionally or not. Here are common sparkle dimmers to watch out for:

- Belittling or talking down to you.
- Blaming you for their mistakes.
- Deflating your mood when you're feeling good about yourself.
- Habitually arriving late or disrespecting your time.
- Taking more than they give.
- Talking badly about you behind your back.
- Failing to show up when you need them most.
- Offering unwarranted, harsh criticism.

MIA'S STORY: DON'T LET SOMEONE ELSE'S NEGATIVITY DIM YOUR SPARKLE

Passed over for a promotion after being at the company for two years, she reached out to a coworker for advice, only to be met with dismissiveness from someone she trusted. That was fuel for the fire. It crushed her confidence until her best friend stepped in: "Why are you letting his bad attitude dictate your worth? Let's plan your next move: It's time to look for other opportunities outside the corporation."

SUBTLE SPARKLE THIEVES

Sometimes, the dimmers aren't external—they're habits and mindsets we let creep in. Here are a few sneaky sparkle thieves and how to take them down:

1. **Gossiping**
   - *The Issue*: Gossip originates in the mind, distorting others' actions and wasting precious time.
   - *New Approach*: Tell yourself, "This is a waste of my energy. I have better things to focus on today."
2. **Daydreaming Without Action**
   - *The Issue*: Fantasizing about a better life without taking steps to create it.
   - *New Approach*: Ask yourself, "What can I change right now to make my life better?" Then, take a single action toward your goal.
3. **All-or-Nothing Thinking**
   - *The Issue*: Viewing life as either amazing or awful, with no in-between.
   - *New Approach*: Remind yourself that life is full of shades of gray. Bumps in the road don't define the whole journey.
4. **Assuming**
   - *The Issue*: Believing you know what someone else is thinking or feeling—and acting on it.
   - *New Approach*: Stop mind-reading. Ask instead, "I thought you might be feeling ____(fill in the blank). Is that true?"
5. **Blaming**
   - *The Issue*: Pointing fingers to avoid looking inward.
   - *New Approach*: Pause and reflect, "Why is this triggering me? What am I really feeling?" Respond with clarity, not emotion.

WHAT RESTORES SPARKLE?

The great news is that sparkle can be rekindled—often with simple, joyful activities. Here are some surefire sparkle boosters:

- Take reflective time in a cozy chair with no distractions.
- Treat yourself to a foot massage.
- Go barefoot. Take a walk in nature and feel the earth beneath your feet.
- Soak in a luxurious bubble bath.

- Lose yourself in a chapter of your favorite book.
- Watch a romantic TV show or a feel-good movie.
- Indulge in creative hobbies like knitting, sewing, or painting.
- Browse the latest styles at your favorite boutique—no pressure to buy.
- Tap into your inner child: grab crayons and a coloring book, or play a nostalgic game.
- Sneak in a fifteen-minute catnap.[*]

These aren't extravagant acts; they're small investments in yourself that pay off in restored energy and joy.

THE BOTTOM LINE

Sparkle isn't just about how you look; it's about how you *feel*. The vibrancy comes from *Living Richly*—physically, emotionally, and spiritually. Guard your sparkle fiercely. Recognize what dims it and take proactive steps to restore it when it fades.

As you move forward, remember that when you sparkle, you inspire others. Your light is contagious.

Living Richly Practice
Your Musical Oasis

Find a quiet spot, free from distractions. Put on some soothing music that uplifts your spirit. Sit comfortably, and either close your eyes or lower them. Let the music draw you into the present moment, melting away the noise of the day. Take a few deep breaths, feeling the air fill your lungs and release any remaining tension with each exhale. Slowly open your eyes, refreshed and peaceful.

---

[*] Helene Lerner, *Time for Me: Self-Care and Simple Pleasures for Women Who Do Too Much,* (Illinois: Simple Truths-Sourcebooks, 2015, 2022), 47.

CHAPTER TAKEAWAYS

- Sparkle is not just about how you look; it comes from an inner glow connected to your vitality.
- Don't let anyone or anything dim your sparkle.
- Keep sparkle boosters at the top of mind and use them when you need a pick-me-up.

NUGGET FROM THE HEART

Approach life with positive expectancy. Say to yourself, *"New good is coming to me now, from known and unknown sources."*

FOR YOUR JOURNAL

1. How have you allowed others to dim your sparkle or take advantage of you? Reflect on how you can set boundaries to protect your energy.
2. Have you participated in gossip or blamed someone recently? What happened, and how did it make you feel afterward?
3. What sparkle-boosting activity will you add to your daily routine to nurture your vitality and joy?

CHAPTER 18

❦

EIGHTY DAYS OF JOY FORMATIONS

Joy is your spiritual birthright. Be open to blessings coming your way.

𝓜 ove through your day with joy in your heart and the unshakable belief that you can handle any challenge. Know too, that blessings are on their way.

Too often, we get caught in the unending loop of responsibilities that diminishes our joy.

Take Brooke, a teacher I know, who is a caregiver to both her mother and young child. Burned out and depleted, she had forgotten what fun felt like. "When was the last time you did something just for you?" I asked her. She hesitated, then admitted, "Not for a long while." I asked what brought her joy. "Tap dancing," she said, though she hadn't danced in ages.

With a little encouragement, she enrolled in a class. The next time I saw her, her face lit up. "I did it!" she beamed. Her spark was back.

As we've explored throughout this book, the secret to a joyful life takes awareness and a willingness to change: transform your thinking. Don't indulge fear, doubt, or negativity—change the channel. One of the best tools for doing that is *Joy Formations.*

WHAT ARE JOY FORMATIONS?

Joy Formations aren't just words; they are affirmations designed to shift your perspective and invite a new mindset. They're daily reminders to see your world through a prosperous lens and embrace the abundance around you.

When you find yourself stuck in a negative loop, Joy Formations can help you reframe your thoughts and recenter your energy.

HOW TO USE JOY FORMATIONS

There are 80 Joy Formations below, one for each day of a transformative journey. Here's how to make the most of them:

1. Start Your Day with Intention. Choose one Joy Formation each morning. Say it out loud before you leave home, and feel its truth resonate in your heart.

2. Keep It Close. Write it down on a slip of paper or store it in your phone. You can glance at it throughout the day, especially when you need a boost.

WITH EVERY STEP, GROWTH AWAITS

This book has been your companion on a journey toward *Living Richly,* authentically, and joyfully. As we conclude, let these Joy Formations guide you in navigating life's challenges and embracing life's opportunities.

EMBRACING THE JOURNEY

1. I move through the discomfort of change and embrace
the life lessons before me.

2. I am willing to change my "story" about how someone should be and see them for who they really are.

3. No matter how small, each change I make builds upon the last; I am creating a strong foundation.

4. We all make mistakes. I learn the lessons and move on.

5. Not everyone is who they say they are. I can accept that on move on.

LIVING AUTHENTICALLY

6. The greatest gift I can give someone is to be my authentic self.

7. Not all knowledge comes from the head; I will listen to my heart more.

8. I trust my intuition because it is connected to the truth.

9. I am heard when I speak from the heart.

10. When I strongly feel something is wrong, I trust my gut.

11. I let people know how I really feel, even if it causes an argument.

12. I act and do not look back. I stop second-guessing myself.

13. Integrity is at the core of courageous conversations and I take part in them.

OWNING YOUR POWER

14. I know that I can handle anything the world throws at me.

15. I put my "big girl" pants on when things get challenging. I am up to the challenge!

16. I will never give up on something I believe in.

17. I pay attention to what someone does—not what they say—and act accordingly.

18. If someone does me wrong, it is because they think very little of themselves.

19. I don't stoop to the level of someone who is hurting.
20. I have little to do with negative people–they drain my energy.
21. I give from an authentic place.
22. I let someone have their say; we can agree to disagree!
23. I don't overspend; there is no lasting joy in that.
24. I am learning to be my own best friend and to praise myself more.
25. My confidence builds when I act. I don't sit and wait.

TAKING INITIATIVE

26. I am resourceful. I know what is needed and take action accordingly.
27. I don't wait for permission; I do what feels right.
28. I stay away from foolishness because I have more important things to do.
29. I don't show up late. I am on time or early!
30. I say "yes" today—who knows where I will be tomorrow.
31. I have a great capacity for joy and look for ways to express it throughout the day.

MAKING AN IMPACT

32. I act when I know I can make a difference.
33. I inspire others to be their best selves.
34. I am a leader and pick my issues. I let my voice be heard.
35. I stand tall and say what's on my mind. My example can help someone else.
36. I lend a helping hand to someone in need.
37. I offer a compliment to an unsuspecting person.
38. I practice kindness to the people around me.
39. I am a light for others who are having their dark moments.

ENJOYING LIFE'S RICHES

40. I know that the best things in life don't cost a cent.

41. I allow myself to receive something wonderful that is totally unexpected.

42. I watch the sunrise at the beginning of the day and connect with its uplifting energy.

43. I take in a child's smile and let it warm my heart.

44. I look for beauty in a person I don't know.

45. Flowers are the jewels of nature, and I delight in them.

46. I get up an hour earlier once a week and do something that brings me joy.

47. I wear my favorite color at least three times a week because it makes me feel good.

48. I whip up a scrumptious meal, sit down at a decked-out table, and make a toast to myself.

49. I dance in my living room when no one is around—just for me!

GOING WITH THE FLOW

50. I practice patience: things happen at the right and perfect time.

51. I live in the moment and do not try to project what will happen in my future.

52. My life is filled with ups and downs. I am learning to ride the wave!

53. I don't sweat the little or big things; nothing is worth my peace of mind.

54. My best is good enough; there is no such thing as perfection!

55. Even when bad things happen, I look for the silver lining.

56. When one door closes, a better one will open. I have faith!

57. Money is not everything, but it helps—I am open to receiving abundance from known and unknown sources.
58. If it is not meant for me, I bless it and let it go.
59. If I can't do something now, it does not mean that I never will. The timing may be off.
60. It's okay not to feel okay.
61. When there are too many obstacles, I question whether I should continue or do something else.
62. My unique destiny is unfolding now. I enjoy the process of seeing it manifest.

LIVING IN COMMUNITY

63. I appreciate our differences and know our common bond.
64. When I am in need, I know that help is available, and I reach out for it.
65. My soul sisters celebrate my successes and share in my losses. They are there for me, no matter what.
66. I will tell one thing to a trusted friend that I have kept secret.
67. I make sure I keep good company.

KNOWING THE POWER OF WORDS AND ACTIONS

68. My words have impact; they can be deadly or inspiring.
69. When I'm upset, I take a pause to process how I am feeling.
70. When in doubt, I don't speak. I wait until I'm clear on what to say.
71. I lower my voice if someone is raising theirs.
72. Listening shows people I care about them.
73. The sound of a voice tells you a lot. I listen to its nuances.

74. I don't make light of a compliment. I take it in.
75. Who is keeping score? I don't compare myself to others because that leads to not enoughness.
76. I give myself some slack—I do my best at any given time.
77. I pay attention to what's bothering me, if it keeps me up at night!
78. Creativity can come from the strangest sources. I stay open and enjoy the ride!

APPRECIATING SILENCE

79. I let go of the noise of the world and appreciate moments of silence.
80. I pause between activities to regroup.

AFTERTHOUGHT

Let the strength, passion, and vitality of the people in this book reignite your sparkle. Their stories are a reminder of what is possible when we *Live Richly*.

At this very moment, you are being called to step into your greatness.

Go in peace, go with power, and go in love.

Living Richly Practice
Closing Meditation

Begin by taking three deep breaths, in through your nose and out through your mouth. With each exhale, let go of any tension, stress, or worry. Now, imagine yourself walking down a country road at night. The air is crisp, and the stars shine brightly above, blanketing the sky like a tapestry of light.

In this moment, you feel an overwhelming sense of peace and gratitude. The stillness around you reflects the calm within. Each step deepens your commitment to using your unique talents to make a difference—not only in your own life but also in the lives of others.

Joy wells up in your heart, pure and unshakable. You feel the richness of life, and with an open heart, you whisper, *Amen.*

NUGGET FROM THE HEART

Joy is a great energizer. It lifts your spirit and turns the ordinary into something extraordinary.

FOR YOUR JOURNAL

1. Think of a recent time when your heart was filled with joy. What happened? Who were you with?
2. How does feeling joyful change your perception of everyday life?

APPENDIX A

GEMS FROM THE LIVING RICHLY TOOLKIT

This bonus section contains practical gems designed to support you when life's road gets bumpy. Reflect on each one, journal your insights, and keep them close when you need a reminder of your resilience and strength.

- Make your **spiritual well-being** a top priority.
- In times of extreme stress, put yourself in intensive self-care. **Treat yourself like someone you deeply love.**
- If you make a mistake, take it in stride. **Next time, you'll know better. Progress, not perfection, is the goal.**
- Focus on what's good, not what isn't going well. **What you focus on grows.**
- Realize that anything that happens—good or bad—can make you stronger. **Life's challenges are your stepping stones.**
- **Detach from toxic people.** Don't let them pull you into their negativity; rise above them.
- See situations that didn't work out as preparation for something better. **There are lessons in our mistakes.**
- Surround yourself with people who affirm you, not bring you down. **You become the company you keep.**

- Follow your heart and stay open to unexpected ways money and abundance can flow into your life. **Creativity and trust open new doors.**
- Live within your means and avoid overspending. **Financial well-being creates emotional peace.**
- Appreciate the *little things* in life, for they are really the *big things*. **Joy is found in simplicity.**

APPENDIX B

THE SMART WOMEN LIVE RICHLY SURVEY: METHODOLOGY AND RESULTS

*I*n my work, I've seen how women are challenged by navigating work, their personal lives, and the endless demands of these tumultuous times.

With these stressors bearing down on us, how do we make wise, intentional choices?

To better understand these challenges, I created *The Smart Women Live Richly Survey*. Women from diverse backgrounds and life stages contributed their voices, offering insights into the obstacles they face and the strategies they use to move through them.

SURVEY METHODOLOGY

The survey, conducted in the fall of 2024, consisted of 26 multiple-choice, open-ended, and demographic questions. The results for each question are presented below.

SURVEY INSTRUMENT

1. What does "Living Richly" mean to you?
99 responses (free-writing)

Answer	Response Percentages
2. Do you believe that Living Richly is mostly dependent on money?	
Yes.	13.1%
No.	33.6%
Partially.	53.3%

3. If you answered yes to the previous question, do you feel that there is a specific dollar amount that would enable you to fully live your "rich lifestyle?"

Yes, and I know what that number is.	10.8%
Yes, but I'm not sure what the amount is.	28.9%
No, I don't think that money would enable that change.	60.2%

4. What impact does showing people the "real you" have on creating a rich lifestyle?

Being myself makes my life feel more expansive.	83.2%
No impact, because a rich lifestyle is about having money.	5.6%
Unsure–I struggle with letting people know me.	11.2%

5. What creates a poverty mentality?

Not appreciating all that I have.	77.1%
Not having enough money.	19.0%
I'm unsure, but I do feel poorer than I would like.	3.8%

6. How has guilt stopped you from Living Richly? Select those that might apply.

I was too concerned about my kids, so I put my needs last.	21.3%
Too concerned with eldercare, I put my needs last.	9.3%
Too concerned with "people pleasing," put my needs last.	39.8%
It hasn't.	39.8%
Other.	13.9%

7. Self-care is essential in living a rich lifestyle. Are you taking enough time out to rest and recharge?

Yes.	58.5%
No.	41.5%

Answer	Response Percentages

8. How often do you practice self-care?
Often, multiple times a week.	47.6%
Sporadically, two or four times a month.	22.9%
I need to do more activities just for me.	29.5%

9. Self-care goes beyond taking care of your physical needs. It's important to be compassionate with yourself as well. How would you describe your inner dialogue?
Positive.	34.6%
Negative.	4.8%
Somewhere in between.	60.6%

10. Have you ever been in a situation where you knew what was needed and that you could provide it, but you held back out of fear of how others might react? If so, where did this happen? Select all that apply.
At work.	37.0%
With family.	35.2%
With friends.	28.7%
Out in public.	31.5%
That hasn't happened to me.	32.4%

11. When you experience situations where you could have acted but did not because you were afraid, do you regret that later on?
Yes.	40.6%
No.	12.9%
Sometimes.	46.5%

12. Imagine you're having a conversation with someone whose opinion of you matters a great deal. Do you think you would act dishonestly so that you might impress them?
Yes.	4.7%
No.	68.2%
Maybe.	27.1%

13. What do you think impresses people the most?
How kind you are.	41.5%
Money and material possessions.	8.5%
Social status.	5.7%
Skill/accomplishment in your career.	24.5%
Other.	19.8%

Answer	Response Percentages

14. How much do you feel your opinion of what it means to live "richly" is influenced by others' money or material possessions?

A great deal.	7.5%
A little.	48.1%
None at all.	44.3%

15. What would your life be like right now if money was not an issue?

All my problems would be solved.	4.8%
A little easier than it is now.	46.7%
It wouldn't change much; the important things would still be the same.	48.6%

16. Are you having enough fun in your life?

Yes.	54.7%
No.	45.3%

17. If not, what gets in the way?

57 responses (free writing)

18. What makes people joyful?

Having wealth.	2.3%
Being able to enjoy the little things in life.	97.7%
A combination of both.	0.0%

19. What brings you the greatest joy?

Being with the people I love.	50.0%
Money.	0.0%
A combination of both.	42.6%
Other.	7.4%

20. Think of what hobbies/pursuits you engage in that might bring you joy. If you are devoting time to them now, how often?

Often, multiple times a week.	46.3%
Sporadically, once or twice a month.	41.7%
Almost never.	12.0%

21. Do you practice gratitude daily?

Yes.	73.8%
No.	26.2%

Answer	Response Percentages
22. Do you use your time efficiently?	
Yes.	27.1%
No.	4.7%
I could do better.	68.2%
23. Do you have a prayer/meditation practice?	
Yes.	55.1%
No.	28.0%
I want one.	16.8%
24. What age range do you fall into?	
20 or under.	9.3%
21-25.	5.6%
26-30.	2.8%
31-35.	1.9%
36-40.	9.3%
41-45.	8.3%
46-50.	7.4%
Over 51.	55.6%
25. What gender do you identify as?	
Female.	94.4%
Male.	5.6%
Other.	0.0%
26. What best describes your current position?	
Unemployed.	1.9%
Student.	12.0%
Freelancer.	5.6%
Entry-level employee.	1.9%
Experienced non-manager.	17.6%
Mid-level manager.	8.3%
Senior-level manager.	8.3%
Business owner.	13.9%
Educator.	3.7%
Stay-at-home parent.	0.9%
Retired.	17.6%
Other.	8.3%

ACKNOWLEDGEMENTS

*T*hank you, Usher Morgan, for believing in this book and recognizing that it was needed during these turbulent times.

Zachary Mattison, my intern—your insights, creativity, and organizational skills are greatly appreciated.

Jennifer Morrison at Mazda for distributing the survey to women at the company, and Leanne McLemore for giving it out to students at New York University.

Sandy Leger, my soul sister—your big smile and encouragement have helped me step into a rich lifestyle.

Marcia Markland, your generous guidance is always welcomed.

INDEX

INDEX

INDEX

ABOUT THE AUTHOR

Helene Lerner is a trailblazing influencer and empowerment expert who has dedicated her career to inspiring individuals to live boldly and authentically. A prolific author, accomplished public television host, Emmy Award-winning executive producer, keynote speaker, and workplace consultant, Helene has built a legacy rooted in uplifting others.

As the founder of the WomenWorking brand, Helene has cultivated a robust presence globally. She is the CEO of Creative Expansions, Inc., a multimedia company with a mission to empower individuals, particularly women and girls, to achieve their full potential.

Helene's expertise has made her a trusted voice in personal and professional development. She has appeared on major national programs such as *Good Morning America*, *The Today Show*, CNN, and Fox News.

With an unrelenting passion for making a difference, Helene continues to inspire individuals across the globe to embrace their power, *Live Richly*, and lead with purpose.

www.ingramcontent.com/pod-product-compliance
Lightning Source LLC
Chambersburg PA
CBHW061352270226
40349CB00006B/51